Jesus and Ourselves
An Alternative Understanding of Christianity

by Michael Roden

Also by Michael Roden:

Songs of the Morning: Meditations for Healing

FREE

JESUS AND OURSELVES

AN ALTERNATIVE UNDERSTANDING OF CHRISTIANITY

MICHAEL RODEN

IP

Infinite Passion Publishing
P. O. Box 340815
Columbus, OH 43234

Jesus and Ourselves:
An Alternative Understanding of Christianity

Published in the United States of America by
Infinite Passion Publishing
P. O. Box 340815
Columbus, Ohio 43234.
(614) 792-0053.

Scripture quotations are from the Revised Standard Version of the
Bible, copyright © 1946, 1957, and 1971, by the Division of
Christian Education of the National Council of the Churches of
Christ in the U.S.A. Used by permission.

The ideas represented herein are the personal interpretation and
understanding of the author and are not necessarily endorsed by
the copyright holder of A Course in Miracles:
The Foundation for Inner Peace, Inc.
P. O. Box 598
Mill Valley, CA 94942-0598.

Library of Congress Catalog Card Number: 96-77328
ISBN: 0-9652996-0-0

10 9 8 7 6 5 4 3 2 1

Printed in the United States of America

TABLE OF CONTENTS

Acknowledgments

Much appreciation to my parents, Jerry and Theodora Roden, who have done much to help make this book possible, in their graciousness, including passing along to me, through their example, some of their great intuitiveness, and a transcendent faith which is quite natural to them.

Thanks to Emila Smith for her golden ideas which give off sparks, and her constant friendship.

Thanks to Dr. Richard Wing for his encouraging and inspirational talks with me; to Joseph H. Yearling, Jr., for his generous assistance and advice; to Kevin Showe for his benevolent help; and to Jack and Lucy Brady for their much-needed continued encouragement.

A special thanks to Sarah Beth and Nicholas Roden for helping keep me by turns grounded and inspired as I wrote this.

Considerable gratitude to my wife, Carol, for her inestimable assistance: her careful editing and her persistent hard work, her artistic taste and her innate wisdom, her friendship and her loveliness, her considerable patience, and her resonant belief and dedication.

Introduction.

A Question of Faith.

Where does faith come from? It comes from beyond our-selves. It comes from beyond anything we have made. When it comes, it comes of its own accord, whenever we are ready for it.

Does faith come to us, or does it draw us to itself? In the Gospel of John (6:44), Jesus states, "'No one can come to me unless the Father who sent me draws him.'" And Jesus also states in that Gospel (12:32), "'and I, when I am lifted from the earth, will draw all men to myself.'"

According to this understanding, therefore, faith is more than a conceptual system to which we must say "yes" or "no." Some-times faith seems to be a sense of deeper significance which is not well-defined nor well-controlled. Sometimes it transcends who we think we are, and takes on a mind, even an identity, all its own. If life itself is more than we think we are, why would not faith be?

Faith is more than we think; it encompasses more than thought. It is also more than we feel. But it brings us a different kind of feeling, different than the kind which normally occupies us. It brings us a feeling which comes from beyond ourselves, a feeling which shows us how much more to life there is beyond what we can normally see and feel. These are the thoughts and feelings which

will prove to be most deeply memorable, and, though they may occur for only the smallest and rarest of moments, these are the thoughts
and feelings which will most fully reflect the full course of our lives.
    Faith is not static, though its riverbed is made of solid rock.
It is fluid in the course it has set. It provides us with unbound thoughts
and timeless feelings, and these carry us through the world, showing
up in our daily lives, in time. But each person may respond to the
same timelessness differently, and differently at different times during the course of life.
    What does it mean to have faith? There are as many an-
swers to this question as there are people to respond to it. Christianity itself is incredibly diverse, made up of many faiths. Christianity
is bigger than each of us, and yet it includes every single one of us.
    Faith is not a belief or a set of beliefs, but is instead a way of
life. It is not something that Jesus requires of us, but something that
Jesus shares with us. Some might say that faith is life itself, but that
we do not know what life is, so we do not know what faith is.

    In this book we will center our discussion about faith on a
man called Jesus. One need not even be a Christian to receive the
faith he brings, the life he inspires. In fact, beliefs, in the sense of
personal opinions or even conventional tenets, may prove to inhibit
faith. For opinions and tenets have a way of interposing themselves
between ourselves and the selflessness of faith, and between ourselves and Jesus. Beliefs are conceptual, for the most part, and they
have a way of keeping us locked into a concept of ourselves. The
faith he brings, on the other hand, is liberating because it comes
from beyond ourselves.
    We will use whatever resources are available to us to learn
of Jesus and the faith he brings, keeping in mind that, in the end, the
faith he brings will come from beyond our learning. Yet it is learning which prepares the way, learning not only from Gospels, and
from other books, but learning from life itself.
    The process itself of study is interesting. For faith provides
its own course of instruction. Whatever is available it will use. And
whatever is available faith will provide. We exclude nothing out of

hand. For faith requires great openness from us; it requires our fullest sense of trust.

We do not discriminate in terms of the ideas we may use. If one has an idea, and if that idea is heartfelt and not merely conceptual, then let that person bring that idea to the table. It is the idea which must prove itself, not the social or religious identity of the person who spoke it.

Is historical Biblical scholarship harmful to faith? The better question is whether it is harmful to conceptions of faith or to faith itself. For though an idea may serve to counteract conceptions of faith, only an idea as vast and as powerful as faith can counteract faith itself. And I have neither seen nor felt such an idea. Even when you think it has fled from your life, faith may reappear, stronger than ever before.

With the historians, we will be searching for Jesus as he was in his earthly life, but this does not mean that we will of necessity exclude the risen Christ. But to know the risen Christ already requires faith, at least initially, and I am writing also for people who have an intuitive interest in faith but who do not yet feel its transcendence. Therefore we center our discussion upon a teacher and example of transcendence in humanness, the man Jesus.

The Gospels can be read so as to find out more about him. There we find, as we peer behind the theology and the faith which radiates from their pages, that Jesus was a man, a human being, whatever else he may be. And we begin to feel that there is something significant about that fact, and about the man himself, and we feel this significance at the very point where his humanity meets and mingles with our own. This being who is now the risen, abstract, and universal Christ once walked the earth, as we do, only with a sense of purpose, of certainty, and of actuality that we do not understand.

There is something significant in the humanness of Jesus, just as there is something significant in the way in which Jesus transcends humanness. It is this transcending of humanness that we refer to when we speak about his "risenness," for we have little clue as to what else it might mean. It seems to be an experience that we cannot yet share. But his humanness: that we already share. We feel that this humanness has the power to draw him closer to us, primarily by drawing ourselves closer to him.

Even as a man, as a human being, Jesus was more than we have ever thought him to be. There may have been no great breach, no great dichotomy, between the Jesus of history and the risen Christ. The breach is probably greater between how we think of him and how he thought of himself. But even that is nothing next to the breach that exists between the way *he* thought of us, as humans, versus the way *we* tend to think of ourselves.

And this is what our forms of faith often seem to be lacking: an appropriately uplifting view of ourselves, a view more like how the human Jesus might have seen us. Historians who study the Bible are helping to get this back by trying to determine what Jesus really said as a human being in contrast to the beliefs and experiences of later Christians as they were made part of his story. We want to learn what he himself had to say, and then, if we can, we will correlate this to what the risen Christ revealed and continues to reveal to his followers.

As a human being, Jesus seems less like an object of faith and more like an example we might follow. What he was and even what he is seems more reachable. And what he taught seems less and less about himself and his special relationship to God and more and more about all of us and about our own relationships, to God and to each other. What he spoke about and how he lived concerns us directly, and it concerns us whether or not we think of ourselves as Christians. For though he taught in a limited area and to a limited group of people during his earthly time, we feel that his teaching was universal enough to speak to and include every one of us. It is to our common humanness, perhaps, that he spoke most often.

Even as a human being, Jesus was compelling. He was able to evoke a deep faith in those who were ready to receive this from him. He was able to inspire human beings to reach beyond themselves for whatever it was he offered them: healing love, saving love, enlightening love. When they had reached out to him in faith, a faith they did not know they had before they heard him, they were reaching out past who they thought they were, and they were seeking to touch the hem of the garment of him who showed them who they were in truth.

But when historians attempt to explain what it was about Jesus that made other human beings believe in him and connect with him as they did, this is where they sometimes come up lacking. For this is a connection which straight history cannot convey. Those who believed in him or who reached out to him had made leaps of faith, from within themselves, where the gravity of history does not operate. Only as the same leap of faith is made today do we find that we have more to go on, and more evidence at hand, in our midst, and within ourselves.

Jesus himself was not merely a historical figure, just as he was not merely a theological figure or an object of worship. He was a human being with depth. And so are we human beings with depth, though we may not realize it until we have "seen" and experienced the reality of this depth. At any rate, even the human Jesus sought to show us that we are more than we think we are.

As human beings with depth, we have an advantage over history and over theology as well. As beings of depth, we are fully capable of self-transcendence. And, because only depth can know depth, we are capable of finding Jesus directly, whenever we are ready to receive such insight.

Any enterprise which has based itself on Jesus—whether it be historical Biblical criticism or literary criticism or even theology—has, wittingly or not, involved itself within the larger enterprise of self-transcending. Therefore theology (for instance) may believe that its task is to immerse itself in words, and to precisely define its constructs in such terms, but it possesses an even greater responsibility. Its greater responsibility involves overcoming itself, particularly when it begins to step into the way of self-knowledge.

Our own responsibility is great. One aspect of our responsibility is to learn all we can, so that we can make effective decisions at the level of depth. We cannot remove this responsibility from ourselves, but we can and have hidden it from ourselves. We cannot insist that we have ceded our responsibility to someone else, whether that someone else be another individual or an institution. For our responsibility will always be our own, no matter to whom or to what we have given it. It is ours; it belongs to us.

Where does faith come from? It comes from beyond ourselves, but also from within ourselves. It comes from beyond anything we have made of ourselves, from beyond any individual identity, social identity, or even religious identity we have made for ourselves. It comes from essentially the same place in us that it came from in Jesus.

It is here in humanness, here in the midst of the world, that these thoughts and feelings of faith are applied. It is here, in the midst of temporality and fleetingness that we learn of the timelessness of eternity. It is here, among our brothers and sisters, friends and strangers, that we learn to apply the teachings of Jesus, and learn to see him in everyone, by letting his truth shine through ourselves.

Chapter One.

Our Relation to Jesus.

To Live and to Believe.

What does it mean to live? What does it mean to be a human being? What does it mean to think and to feel? What is our relation, if any, to the ultimate source of life, to God? These are questions of self-knowledge, questions pertaining to and therefore questions in search of self-knowledge of a very elemental kind.

We must delve deep to answer such questions, deeper than we normally go. For most of us, these questions will remain unasked and unanswered. Most of us don't seem to believe that we are entitled to ask such basic questions, let alone to receive answers to them. But it may well be our responsibility to ask them. If we accept the theologies and the philosophies and the mythologies that have been handed down to us simply because they have been handed down to us, having worked perhaps for people in the past, then we will probably see no need to ask such questions nor to have them answered. But once we have stepped into the stream, that stream is no longer simply tradition, for us, but is more similar to life itself.

Questions which involve us, which engage us, and which will not leave us alone, might be referred to as core questions or core concerns. They might be referred to as existential questions, or as questions of the whole person, or as questions of the heart. They might be referred to as questions tending toward self-knowledge.

There is a place within us where such questions are asked naturally. They arise of themselves—in effect, they ask themselves, at least until they are answered. That is the place to which we seek to go. It is that place to which Jesus sought to lead us. That place is within ourselves.

Religion in particular is supposed to relate to life. It is supposed at least to seek out possible answers to these questions of self-knowledge. Perhaps religion has involved itself in secondary, non-essential matters for the most part. Yet does its original purpose, and its original attraction, still exist inside ourselves.

Inner life and experience was not always separated from outward existence as it is today. Religion itself was part of life before it had ever become part of culture. Because it related to life itself, religion could not be boxed in or boxed out. From the surface, it is easy to confuse the practice of religion with religion itself, which is not so much a set of behaviors or even beliefs as much as it is a way of living, because it involves relating with others and questioning oneself.

Religion's original question was: What does it mean to live? This question has been replaced by a more conceptual one. Much of religion is currently concerned with: What do we believe? Often, its concern is with distinguishing itself from other believers. It is as if having life were already known, and that we already know what it means to live. Yet, belief for Jesus seems to have been much more than a way of conceptualizing, or of adhering to a rigid code of laws or beliefs; it was a way of living, which includes feeling and relating to God and to other people. For Jesus, to believe was to live, and to live quite effectively, and probably quite joyfully as well.

Jesus came to teach people and to show people, not what it means to be religious, but what it means to live. For Jesus, and for much of his culture, religion and life were interwoven; they were seamless. They were one not because the authorities had so decreed it, nor because religious and political authorities were one and the same in first-century Judaism. Rather, religion was one with life because, in the minds of the people, religion asked and provoked answers to questions which were essential to life.

Because it often fails to do so, we forget that religion has the power to captivate a person. One need not go out and seek to capture religion. Approached ever-so-hesitantly from within, religion can still captivate and draw us in. It can still speak to our deepest mind and reflect our deepest heart.

The Distance Between Us.

Although religion at its best asks questions which concern the depth within ourselves, such questions cannot be answered by ourselves alone. Religion is not entirely an interior phenomenon; it must enter the world, as each person must enter the world. It must look to the world, at least for application, if not confirmation, of the ideas spoken to or by one's inner depth. And it must share itself in some way, through words or, more effectively, through example, teaching not only how to live but what it means to live. Religion works in the world, in other words, when it provides us with a sense of deep significance.

Yet the world of our daily lives seems so far from religion, far from internal significance. More specifically, our daily world, including our religion, seems so far from Jesus, from his words as well as from his life, from his teaching and his example. Why? Why does there seem to be such a great gulf between us?

Let us begin by asking why *we* have set Jesus apart. Our theologies have set him apart; they have removed him to and above the skies, where we no longer can see him, while we have remained earthbound. This makes the distance between Jesus and ourselves seem to be a self-imposed one, based, ironically, on our beliefs about him.

Obviously if anyone deserves the utmost respect for the way in which he lived his life, particularly considering the circumstances of his life, what he managed to do without worldly resources, the things he taught and how he taught them, and the way in which he faced impending death, Jesus is a person deserving of such respect. But the adulation that we have given him has elevated him far beyond our reach. We have forgotten to allow ourselves to be raised with him, so that we can see him, not as towering above us, but rather as a teacher and as a friend, and as one of us.

Our adulation of him has centered itself on his risenness, but even this need not cause us to forget the teaching and example which led to such risenness. We have quite a bit of information about his earthly life, compared to what we have of other figures of his time, and yet we do not use this information to determine why he inspired such an outpouring of faith even during his earthly life.

The distance between Jesus and ourselves is not the distance of thousands of years; it is not the distance of time. Nor is the distance between us the distance of culture; this too can easily be overcome or overlooked. Even the difference of effectiveness—the distance between what he could accomplish versus what we have accomplished—does not quite capture the essence of our distance from Jesus.

The real distance between Jesus and ourselves is a psychological distance. It is a difference in the way we think, about him and about ourselves as well. For how we think about ourselves has far-reaching effects: it affects our relations with others, and it affects our relation with God.

How we think about Jesus has affected how we think about ourselves, and how we think about ourselves has affected how we think about Jesus. We have constructed an inverse relationship between him and ourselves: he is greatest, we are least; he is perfect, we are eternally imperfect. We have often thought of ourselves as nothing in comparison with him. But we who see and emphasize his divinity have a tendency to forget how strongly he emphasized his relation to humanity. He has said that he could be found in the least, in those who were less than perfect in the eyes of the world, in those same lowly people with whom he socialized during his lifetime on earth. He joined himself with them in his life. Yet we do not look for him there, just as we do not look for him in ourselves.

He turned away no one. It is we who have turned away from him, we who have stretched out an impassable distance between Jesus and ourselves. We are the ones who have placed him out of our range. We are the ones who have positioned ourselves lower than he who was himself a little higher than the angels.

We can best look at him if we do not hide our faces from him. We can sit at his feet and learn from him, and even love him without adoring him. For we must allow him to humble himself to us as well, as he himself would have done in his earthly life.

Union or Separation?

The earliest Christologies, the earliest theologies pertaining to him, tended to be participative. Jesus was centrally connected with believers; their lives were conjoined with his. Believers in him and in what he could accomplish were spoken of as sharing his Spirit and something of his life.

The Gospel of John employs, among others, images of vine and branches—"He who abides in me, and I in him, he it is that bears much fruit, for apart from me you can do nothing" (John 15:5)— and of oneness (John 17:20-24) in expressing the unitive relation of Jesus with those who followed him.

Paul the Apostle imagined the body of Christ to have been a spiritual body made up of all believers, each with his or her individual purpose within the whole, with Jesus himself at the head (Ro. 12:4-5; 1 Co. 12:12). He spoke of Christ being in the believer (2 Co. 13:5; Gal. 2:20; Col. 1:27; Ro. 8:10) and of believers being in Christ (Ro. 8:1) and one in Christ (Gal. 3:28), and he spoke of their having the mind of Christ (1Co. 2:16).

Such participative and unitive images stress essential connection with Jesus rather than distance between him and ourselves. Early believers were closer to Jesus not only physically, or in terms of time and place; they were closer to him because they felt closer; they experienced a closeness and a union with him that tenets and conceptual beliefs can neither construct nor fully convey. They were close enough to him in their minds and in their hearts to be joined with him, and the images they used to express their belief expressed this oneness.

Ironically, the same Paul and John who gave us these unitive and participative images of Jesus and ourselves are those early followers who are considered most responsible for the long-standing divide between Jesus and ourselves. For they, to an even greater extent than had the other apostles and evangelists, had separated Jesus from the rest of humankind by placing him in an order of one, an order of being to which only he belonged.

Rather than dissect the theologies of Paul and John in order to determine what their writings really say about the relation between Jesus and ourselves, in this book we will try to capture the spirit of these early theologies by going directly to Jesus himself. We will go first and primarily to the most historical documents we have about Jesus—according to the general agreement of most historians, the Gospels of Mark, Matthew, and Luke—to see if we can glean from them what the relation between Jesus and ourselves is supposed to have been, from Jesus' vantage point. At the same time we will try to find out what kind of life Jesus was bringing us.

The records alone will not tell us all we need to know. We use the records, but the records are not to be the final word. If we simply read the records, without applying them to ourselves, without drawing from them the depth of self-knowledge they contain, then we are simply reading the words. We need to read them with the same spirit with which they were spoken, or written, or inspired. In other words, the experience of reading these words should prove to be indistinguishable from the reading of our own soul, or the Word which has been placed within our heart.

We read the words, as with Paul Tillich, to learn about and to encounter "the living person *behind* the texts from the historian's reconstruction *out of* the text" (in Gilkey, 321). And we read the text, as per Stanley Romaine Hopper (161), as if we were reading "exam questions in self-understanding." For in that way, besides finding out about Jesus, we may come to learn about other living persons behind the text: ourselves.

Ideally, a book about Jesus, particularly an inspired one such as a Gospel, will reveal as much about ourselves as it will about him. For Jesus has a way of bringing us full–circle and back around to ourselves. It is impossible to hold ourselves apart from him, for we find that he will not let us. To talk about him, even to think about him, is to involve ourselves with him. But to believe in him is to participate with him in a new kind of being.

How Human Was He?

Theology has come up with a balanced solution to the "problem" of the relation of Jesus' divinity with his humanity. That is the solution debated and finalized by Church Councils over a thousand years ago, and accepted by most Christians ever since. That solution is that Jesus was *fully divine* and at the same time *fully human*, a wonderfully paradoxical and potentially non-conceptual solution.

But for the most part the theological answers of the past have obscured the relation between Jesus and ourselves, by having emphasized the differences, rather than the similarities, between us. If Jesus was at one time *fully* human, then he was at one time not entirely unlike us. But we have taken his story to be the story of someone fully different, and so we have not learned all that we could from him.

It is because of what he did with his humanness, perhaps despite his humanness, that causes us to think of him as a man set apart from the rest of humanity and set apart from ourselves. The reason we have interpreted him to be more than human, and more than ourselves, is that we could not fit him into our definition of humanness. And so we created a separate category for him.

Once we realized that he did not fit into our definition of humanness, there are two ways we could have gone. One way, the way we in fact went, is to create a separate, higher category for Jesus, and to interpret him as having been of a separate order of being. But the way we have neglected may be the more significant way for us to go; this other way would be to see Jesus as having stretched, expanded, perhaps even obliterated our definition of our own humanness. This way of thinking would change not only the way we see and think and feel about Jesus, but also it would change the way we see and think and feel about ourselves and about all other human beings. Once we have felt this change of mind it becomes possible to see Jesus, or the risen Christ, in all beings, even in the least within society, as he himself counseled we do.

This way of thinking about Jesus (and his humanness) also has the advantage of making him more significant to our lives, not only to our beliefs. Therefore all of our beliefs, not only our beliefs about him, but also those about ourselves and others, are affected by his humanness.

Belief, even higher belief, begins with common ground. We already believe in our own humanness. No great leap is necessary from that belief to the insight that, for Jesus, humanness was more than we have ever assumed it to have been.

We have assumed that Jesus came down to earth to show us what it means to be divine. That may well be highly meaningful, but it does not contain the full significance of Jesus for our own lives. For Jesus, as a *fully* human being, also shows us what it means to be a human being to the fullest; in a sense, he reveals to us what it means to be ourselves, and what it means to live.

What it Means to be Human.

We have seen him as great, as perfect, as ideal—and yet we have expected so little from him, so little for ourselves. We have expected nothing that we can actually feel, nothing that we can ourselves experience, nothing which provides a more-than-conceptual certainty about God or even about our own salvation. We haven't even expected to understand him very well—neither his teaching nor his life, neither his divinity nor his humanness—nor to understand ourselves at anything approaching a deeper level.

If we want a theology or any kind of understanding which is more than speculation, more than educated guesswork, then we will need to come to self-knowledge. Self-knowledge stands behind all the great humanistic disciplines: philosophy, theology, psychology, artistic expression. Self-knowledge is their central nervous system, that which animates and vitalizes them, that which organizes and re-organizes them, and that which provides their certitude. For it is only as we know ourselves that we are able to know anything or anyone else.

We can think of Jesus mythologically and still derive nothing significant from him. We can think of him theologically, and develop a precise and well-defined system around him, but we still may not know him enough to understand him. In either case, we may not know ourselves well enough to understand him.

For we have spun off doctrines with our conceptual minds and have forgotten that significance is more similar to a feeling, a subjective experience, than it is to a concept or construct. There is something vital in Jesus' teaching, in Jesus himself, and in ourselves that has been missed. In fact, that which is most vital in him and his teaching may be that which is most vital in ourselves; if we do not know it in ourselves, where it is so close to us, then how are we ever going to find it in him or in anyone else?

It is through a process of correlation (or co-relation, relation together) with Jesus that we come to know him: he becomes clearer in our minds as we come to know ourselves. Likewise, as we come to understand him and his teaching, we become clearer to ourselves.

The story of Jesus is the story of a human being. We reiterate this not to lessen the status of Jesus in any way, but to begin to raise the status of our own lives, of having been given life, in our minds. For Jesus was a human being who forever changed what it means to be a human being, and, surpassing that, he was a human being who changed forever what it means to live.

Jesus changed what it means to live by having undergone a change or transformation within himself. And yet, however great the change that he himself underwent, Jesus the human being is already related to ourselves by virtue of our common humanness. It is our shared humanness that allows us to follow his teaching and his example in regard to how to live on earth while drawing close to God and closer to others. It is our shared humanness which draws us that much closer to his risenness, his life.

Perhaps at its highest level, humanness begins to transcend itself. Perhaps to be fully human means more than to have tremendous potential; perhaps it means to take responsibility for that potential and to begin fulfilling that potential. Perhaps to be fully human means to be more like Jesus.

If we ourselves are human and if Jesus himself was also once human, then somehow humanness seems less limited and less limiting, less confined and less confining, and more open to God and to others, than we had previously thought. As God, Jesus makes us rethink God, and our relation to God. But as a human being, Jesus makes us rethink ourselves.

Chapter Two.
Jesus Himself.

And passing along by the Sea of Galilee, he saw Simon and Andrew the brother of Simon casting a net in the sea; for they were fishermen. And Jesus said to them, 'Follow me and I will make you become fishers of men.' (Mark 1:16-17).

And in the morning, a great while before day, he rose and went out to a lonely place, and there he prayed. And Simon and those who were with him pursued him, and they found him and said to him, 'Every one is searching for you.' And he said to them, 'Let us go on to the next towns, that I may preach there also; for that is why I came out.' And he went throughout all Galilee, preaching in their synagogues and casting out demons. (Mark 1:35-39).

And he came to Nazareth, where he had been brought up; and he went to the synagogue, as his custom was, on the Sabbath day. And he stood up to read; and there was given to him the book of the prophet Isaiah. He opened the book and found the place where it was written,
'The Spirit of the Lord is upon me,

because he has anointed me to preach good news
        to the poor.
He has sent me to proclaim release to the
        captives
and recovering of sight to the blind,
to set at liberty those who are oppressed,
to proclaim the acceptable year of the Lord.'
And he closed the book, and gave it back to the attendant,
and sat down; and the eyes of all in the synagogue were
fixed on him. (Luke 4:16-20).

Preface.

What is there to say about Jesus himself which has not already been said? After two thousand years of theology, and a couple of hundred years of diligent scholarship on the historical Jesus, have we not exhausted all there is to consider about this man? Is there anything we have yet to uncover about Jesus which we do not already know?

And yet, how well do we really know him? Isn't the information we possess about him, valuable though it may be, at least once-removed from the spirit of the person himself? How difficult it is to know anyone from the outside!

At times it seems that we know just enough about Jesus to confuse ourselves about who he really was. Even historical scholarship, which seeks out the pebbles of historical fact from a small sea of information, has not formed a consensus as to who Jesus really was. A cynic might insist that each person, scholar or not, sees in him exactly what she or he intends to see.

The more optimistic view might be that we, as honest searchers, see in him exactly what we need at the moment we find it in him. Perhaps this happens through no fault of our own—indeed, it may be more a function of grace of some kind.

The point I am making here is that there are many faces we meet on the road to Jesus, each more convincing than the last. Not one of the faces we meet in our journey may be the true one, the face of the real person, then or now. But each one that we meet tells us something new, not only about him, but about ourselves as well. Perhaps the best we can hope for is that, by the end of our journey, at least the face we look *from* is a true one.

Background.

The question is: What do we know about Jesus? What has historical Biblical scholarship taught us? What can our own insight tell us about him? And what can the resulting understanding of him teach us about ourselves?

Very little of his early background comes down to us as having been especially memorable; next to nothing of his formative years has come down to us. He grew up in Nazareth, a tiny, rural Galilean village. His father may or may not have been a carpenter; Jesus may or may not have followed in his father's trade. His mother was named Mary; he may or may not have had brothers and sisters. Jesus may or may not have visited Jerusalem (or any other large city in the general area) while he was growing up. He may or may not have been influenced by surrounding Greek ideas as well as by Jewish ones.

This is about as close as we can get to his early background. What we know about him consists of probably part of a year, or parts of two or three, from his later, more public life, that part of his life he spent teaching and healing. We have nothing written directly by him. Most of his own sayings and stories had probably been passed down through oral traditions before they were recorded on papyrus; only decades later were these sayings and stories edited and compiled into the form of the Gospels with which we are familiar.

Our primary sources for information about Jesus are the Gospels of Matthew, Mark, Luke, and John, Thomas also, if we include that non-canonical Gospel as one with historical information about his teaching. Each of these Gospel writers, compilers, editors, interpreters (for they were all of these), looked back on the life of Jesus through the lens of theological and mythological reflection, and through eyes which had already been influenced by the faith they were writing about. The Gospels were written from the standpoint of faith in order to enhance that faith and to provide further substance for it.

We can detect a specific theological predisposition and agenda which runs through each Gospel. Mark, it seems, wanted to present Jesus' teaching and healings in the context of, and climaxing with, his crucifixion. Matthew presented the sayings and healings of Jesus which had come down to him in context of the ancient Hebrew scriptures and the righteousness he found therein. Luke emphasized the compassion in the Lord Jesus' teaching. John provides us with a universally glorified, yet incredibly selfless, Jesus. The recently discovered Gospel of Thomas presents sayings of Jesus in the context of a somewhat mystical saving *gnosis,* knowledge and experience.

The point, made over and over again by historians, is that the Gospels are not pure historical records. Each Gospel not only shifts the emphasis, even if ever so slightly, but tints the facts to fit that emphasis. There is a core of shared beliefs, certainly among the canonical Gospels, but their differences are striking and at times profound. These differences indicate that, even from within the early outlines of creed and eventually canon, there never had been just one right way to view and interpret Jesus, his life, his teaching, his risenness, or the nature of the transformation his life was able to impart. Once again, each person receives from him what one is ready to receive.

Historians tell us that, overall, perhaps the major difference between the Jesus that the Gospels present and Jesus himself is that Jesus' real message was not about himself but about God (e.g., Borg 1994, 29). Beneath the layers of tradition which can be seen to have been appended to the sayings and healing stories, a stark figure appears, as if from out of nowhere; he teaches and heals, he befriends outcasts, develops a following, and then he disappears just as suddenly. What was the message that he himself left behind, as opposed to the ones his followers, sometimes fervently, sought to apply to him? This task of sorting-out is that which historical Bible scholars have taken upon themselves.

Historians provide information, nearly all of it subject to debate, but they do so on the basis of a sort of common logic. They provide reasons for their conclusions, and they are these reasons which might be questioned, at least some of the time. But the unraveling of the glorious tapestry that has been woven around the central figure of Christianity can itself result in a glorious, perhaps startlingly glorious, moment of encounter. There was a man behind all that faith, and that man is not only intriguing; he was, to some extent, one of us.

The theological thread will not remain unwoven, however, for something extraordinary happened, to this man or to his disciples or to both, which changed forever the way he would be seen and remembered. After suffering the fate of a common criminal or leader of a revolt, and the apparent shame that accompanied this, he was, as the theologians say, "vindicated." This meant to his followers that God had not left him alone, that God had uplifted him, had raised him, from nothingness to life, a life they now could see. This extraordinary happening was read and then written back into the life of Jesus (e.g., Meier 1991, 213), and it gave a whole new meaning to his life and a whole new significance to his teaching and healing. Those who "saw him," after his time on earth, had glimpsed the countenance of Heaven; they had glimpsed the power of God to work through him who used to be a human being, and their friend.

Necessary Assumptions.

We have all made certain assumptions about Jesus. Some of our assumptions depend upon the extent of our experience, some on the extent of the information we have made available to ourselves. To think about Jesus at all is to make or at least to believe certain assumptions about him. To assume anything about his motivation, whether this is done mythologically or theologically or historically or psychologically—and it is done all the time—is to enter the domain of Jesus' self-consciousness. It is a precarious task, subject to error, but it is done all the time, most often unconsciously.

Any time we interpret his teaching to mean certain things, we make certain assumptions about him and certain assumptions about ourselves. To accept the conclusions of historical Bible scholars is to make certain assumptions, just as to accept the Gospels' interpretations as historical or even theological truth is to make (or share) certain assumptions. Any way we look, it seems, we cannot escape making these assumptions. Therefore, it is important to come to terms with what our assumptions are.

Do we assume, with some scholars, that everything that has ever happened must have a naturalistic cause, or series of them, and a naturalistic meaning? Or do we assume, with some people of faith, that the Gospel writers never let their own beliefs and theologies creep into their compositions—that everything they wrote is straight from the hand of God?

Perhaps we assume that Jesus knew at all times what his life and teaching would mean to followers thousands of years hence. Or we assume that he knew exactly what form his vindication and glorification would take. It may be safer to assume with the historians that he may not have known, that his limited knowledge would not have told him that, but that he instead had an inner sense that things would work out, a hope and more than a hope: faith, belief, trust in God, and only from these: knowledge, certainty.

It is particularly important to consider our assumptions when we consider that those theologies and doctrines which developed about him after his time on earth, though perhaps quite valid in and of themselves, rarely reach all the way back to Jesus himself. The result is that what we believe about Jesus is not likely to be what Jesus believed about himself. Again, we cannot escape making our own or accepting others' interpretations about his teaching and his inner life.

Because theology has so influenced our views of him, it is difficult to believe that, at the time Jesus walked the earth, there was no Christological formula, no Trinitarian formula, and no talk of his having been born as a king. All Jesus had to back him up was a sense of personal rightness, some sense of his own mission, and the necessary effectiveness to embark upon it.

Something about him.

Obviously there was something about the person Jesus which lent itself to mythology. Mythology may be as valid a way as any of trying to explain him, for, being a way of explanation which has the capacity to look beneath the surface (via images and symbols which are not consciously chosen) for its significance, mythology has seemed to fit him well. However it has the potential for being greatly misunderstood. For mythological explanation is not historical explanation. Coming from an entirely different place than historical explanation, mythology picks up where the historical explanation leaves off, perhaps because it must leave off.

Mythology has placed a bright star above him at his birth. To look through historical annals for a real star, or conjunction of planets, or other heavenly body, is to miss the point. The point of using mythology at all is to say that he is more than we have made of him, and that he will continue to be more than we can make of him. Each of the elements in the myth which seeks to explain him is a symbol of something which stands beyond explanation.

What is most helpful about mythological and poetic symbols is that they can and often do mean many things at once. They cannot be confined to our usual way of thinking about things. They are not confined to a single correct interpretation. They can serve as symbols of a different kind of experience than that with which we are familiar, and they can even serve to bring that experience if we remain open to it.

Historically, the myth does not fit; but mythologically, the myth fits perfectly. Even the more conservative historical Biblical scholars agree that one need not accept the myth as reality to accept the reality of the myth. They picture a Jesus who had been born near his home, in Nazareth, without fanfare, like a normal child. It was something later in his life that made him what he was. In some way, scholars assert, Jesus developed. He may not have developed in an ordinary way, to have developed into such an extraordinary person. There was something about him, forces at work which may not have been discerned or disclosed when he walked the earth, which made him who and what he was. It is this *something* that the myth helps to account for.

Even as a human being, there was something about him which inspired faith in God. People believed in him as well, but not because they were told that they should; rather, they believed in him because he inspired them. Some were willing to drop everything, including their former lives, their former occupations, even their families, in order to follow him—him, the human being!

The people of his time followed him not because they had heard he had been born beneath a shining star but rather because, human though he was, he had somehow derived an effectiveness which they believed to have come from God. This effectiveness could be heard in his words, seen in his actions and in his general demeanor, and, perhaps most significantly, this effectiveness could be felt in the feelings he seemed to evoke in them. As A. N. Wilson (157) states:

> People flocked to him, not merely because his healing was effective, but because they believed that within the experience of healing, they had come to understand the love of their Creator. That is why Jesus, in common with other healers, proclaimed the forgiveness of the sick person's sin.

There was something about him, even as a human being, which made people believe that they were indeed forgiven when he told them they were forgiven. There was something about him, even as a human being, which made people believe that they were truly healed of their illness when he told them they were healed. Let us search the Scriptures, along with the historians, in order to find out what it was about him, and within him, as a human being, that people believed in, and how we might be able to get it back.

Jesus' General Characteristics.

Let us begin with a basic assumption about Jesus: that he had a sense of mission, a sense of where he was going, though not necessarily a divine and cosmic plan consciously in mind. But it was a mission nonetheless, a sense of calling, similar to, though probably stronger than, what any of us might have at one time or another, a deeper sense that he was meant for something more.

What is a sense of calling but a desire to do more, a deep-seated yearning that one has found a way to fulfill? What is a sense of mission but a calling which has grown into a life-transforming purpose? Where does all this desire and yearning and sense of purpose emanate from except from deep within a person? It must prove itself to be a deep, abiding calling if it is to grow into a mission. We can see from what he did and said that Jesus felt a great connection with other people. And yet it was Jesus' particular sense of mission, perhaps the overwhelming power of his desire to fulfill his mission and to help others, which led him to walk independently, to go his own way.

Such a road can probably grow lonely at times, even with people flocking to him. We see in the Gospels evidence of what were probably painful periods of estrangement from others, including his own family. After he had exorcised demons in his native village for instance:

> And when his family heard it, they went out to seize him, for people were saying, 'He is beside himself.' And the scribes who came down from Jerusalem said, 'He is possessed by Be-el´zebul, and by the prince of demons he casts out the demons.' (Mark 3:21-22).

Likewise, those who had known him before he began to put his mission into practice did not know what to think of him, and the effectiveness of his teaching and his healings, as in Matt. 13:54-56:

> . . . coming to his own country he taught them in their

synagogue, so that they were astonished, and said, 'Where did this man get this wisdom and these mighty works? Is not this the carpenter's son? Is not his mother called Mary? And are not his brothers James and Joseph and Simon and Judas? And are not all his sisters with us? Where then did this man get all this?'

That is the question we want to ask here: Where did this man get all this? For that, we continue to look inside, toward his general characteristics.

Eventually, Jesus came to be associated with the greatest living prophet of the time (before Jesus). But Jesus' sense of independence would not allow him to stay long with his early mentor, John the Baptist. Later, he was asked about his much different personal style from the ascetic Baptist, for Jesus was often seen "eating and drinking" with people, so that people started to call him "'a glutton and a drunkard, a friend of tax collectors and sinners!'" (Luke 7:34). Jesus' response to this accusation was simply that "'wisdom is justified by all her children'" (v. 35), which gives a slight indication that Jesus may have seen himself in a somewhat philosophical sense as one of a number of the children of Wisdom, all working toward the same end, but in markedly different ways.

If he was a prophet, he was more also. If he was a sage, he was more as well. No one category fits him, as the evangelist knew when he wrote that Jesus was "'greater than Solomon'" (a sage) and "'greater than Jonah'" (a prophet) (Luke 11:31, 32). Nothing can confine him, just as nothing can confine the feeling that he evoked in those who looked to him for what he had to give.

Jesus' initial sense of calling and of mission seems to have developed into a remarkable sense of certainty. He knew God's will and he felt God's power; he was willing to impart this will and power through healings and miracles, if asked. He spoke with authority, teaching about God and about how people might be drawn closer to God. It is his sense of inner authority that stands behind the observable authority of his way of teaching. And it is his sense of authority which apparently helped to make him an effective healer and teacher.

Jesus had a *sense* of personal authority—a subjective feeling of authority. It was not the type of authority which would have been recognized by the authorities of the world, for it did not come from the world. It came from no institution; it was probably recognized at first only by him, and accepted at first only by those poor and lost souls who had nowhere else to go, no one else to which to turn (Dunn, 1992, 56). Yet, as C. H. Dodd (49) comments, "Authority it was, with no backing of official position or traditional prestige, to say nothing of legal sanctions or the ultimate sanction of force." To all appearances, all that Jesus had to back up his authority was himself and his effectiveness.

James D. G. Dunn (1975, 79) states that the basis behind Jesus' authority was "not the self-confidence of massive erudition deriving from rabbinic schooling . . ., but a powerful certainty of a direct and unmediated kind." In other words, Jesus' remarkable authority was derived from his remarkable inner experience. Dunn (1977, 186) also states that Jesus' "well-spring of authority was not the law, the fathers, the tradition or the rabbis, but his own certainty that he knew the will of God."

Jesus introduced some of his oracles or sayings with the phrase, "Amen, I say to you...," or "Truly, I say to you...". Raymond E. Brown (70) notes that this is an example of Jesus' having placed his own authority—an authority derived from first-hand experience—behind his words, rather than proclaiming, "Thus saith the Lord...," as a traditional prophet would have done. Moreover, it could be, as Stevan L. Davies (166) asserts, that Jesus had been speaking *from* and *as* the Spirit of God, and not as himself, whenever he spoke in such an authoritative manner. It may be that such an authoritative and independent identity as Jesus spoke from could come only from selfless experience.

The selflessness of Jesus' experience is, according to Davies (139), reinforced by the selfless and "antiegocentric injunctions" in a great many of his teachings. These would include such sayings as "'So the last will be first, and the first last'" (Matt. 20:16), and "'He who is greatest among you shall be your servant; whoever exalts himself will be humbled, and whoever humbles himself will be exalted'" (Matt. 23:11-12).

In a similar vein, it was Jesus' saying in Matt. 10:40, "'He who receives you receives me, and he who receives me receives him who sent me,'" which prompted John E. Smith (80) to state that Jesus could be seen as a "self-negating medium that reveals God in the very act of setting itself aside."

Also, John A. T. Robinson (1984, 164) writes that the Gospel of John emphasizes or brings out the inner experience of Jesus, which had only been hinted at in the other Gospels. And this inner experience of Jesus is seen by that Gospel as having had its basis in selflessness, so that Jesus is seen as transparent to his Father, as in John 14:9: "'He who has seen me has seen the Father.'" And, as Jesus continually states in that Gospel, his teaching and all his works come from a Source beyond himself, as in John 7:16, in which Jesus proclaims, "'My teaching is not mine, but his who sent me.'" Certainly, Robinson (166) states, such assertions as that in John 8:58, "'Truly, truly, I say to you, before Abraham was, I am,'" cannot be taken as self-assertions of the human Jesus; Jesus made these statements, if at all, from a greater identity within him which he knew through experience.

What He Had to Give.

Jesus accepted the religious tradition into which he was born, but he used that tradition creatively. He had done this simply by seeing it differently, by changing its focus. Whereas the thrust of the tradition had seemed to many of its authorities to focus on lawfulness, on what Marcus J. Borg (1994, 50) calls the political "purity system," Jesus focused his religion instead upon subjective feeling and internal experience. Jesus brought this feeling, already there within Judaism, front and center. He made it or discovered it to be the primary characteristic of God, at least within his own mind and experience.

It was because this feeling was the primary characteristic of God that Jesus went about forgiving those who were considered sinners under the law, including them into his vision of the kingdom of God. It was because this feeling was the prime characteristic of God that Jesus was certain he was able to heal people with the mere suggestion of this feeling. And it was because this feeling was felt by Jesus to be God's predominant attribute that Jesus felt entitled to live and to move among the people with God at his side, providing him with what he needed to teach about this feeling.

This feeling was, of course, love, the love of a Father for his children. At the least, this image of fatherly love implies that the love of God is no less strong than the love of the most loving of human fathers. The eye of the Law is not always bearing down upon you, the image seems to say; rather, they are the eyes of love which you should feel when you consider that God sees you.

To feel the love of God is a somewhat different experience than to feel His moral approbation or approval. For the God of law always seems to be judging, weighing our behavior. See God differently and you will see yourself differently; you will see the world differently as well. For one may live under the Law, not by following and "multiplying rules," (Dunn 1992, 91) but by living with the spirit and the leading of love.

One need look no farther to find the key to Jesus' inner being. It is this feeling which unites the man with the myth he became, and this feeling which is the locus of the salvation he brings, no matter what word or act we may find this feeling in. It is this feeling which Jesus passed along to his followers. And it is this same feeling that comes down to us today as the most predominant and distinguishing of his characteristics, no matter how we understand him otherwise to have been.

The Cornerstone of His Characteristics.

In those days Jesus came from Nazareth of Galilee and was baptized by John in the Jordan. And when he came up out of the water, immediately he saw the heavens opened and the Spirit descending upon him like a dove; and a voice came from heaven, 'Thou art my beloved Son; with thee I am well pleased.' (Mark 1:9-11).

Jesus obviously had an experience of God. God was close to him because Jesus felt God inside him. God's power and His very nature (as forgiving, for example) were revealed through him, because he was transparent to God.

But what is not often discussed in relation to Jesus' experience is how his experience might also be the foundation for the way he perceived the world and its people. Jesus drew close to God by experiencing Him differently than had been done in the past. Likewise, he drew close to people by experiencing and perceiving them differently.

Something happened, probably at the time of his baptism by John in the waters of the Jordan River, perhaps before and after as well. Experience came to him. God and the people on earth would never be quite the same, at least to him.

Jesus needed to be alone in the wilderness to pray and to learn how to hear and to follow Spirit. He emerged from the wilderness with something to teach and with much to give. He walked from village to village in his native Galilee drawing people to his vision of God and revealing to them, through firsthand experience, the love God was and is.

Jesus apparently wanted to impart this experience of God. He could talk about the love of God, he could convince people of God's forgiveness, and he could manifest the power of this love. But the only way he could lead people toward the experience of God was by leading them away from their usual perception of the world (ACIM).

This is why he taught that the least (in the world's eyes) would be the greatest in the kingdom of God, and this is why the least in the kingdom of God would be greater than the greatest in the world (Luke 7:28). For to enter the kingdom of God is to enter a realm of experience unlike anything in the world. Because of his experience, Jesus may have felt himself to be one of the first to enter the kingdom of God as he envisioned it.

As Dunn (1977, 189) infers, this experience in Jesus was not quite the same as that enthusiastic experience which characterized the early churches. It was not quite so outer-oriented or centered on outward displays. In some ways it was more below the surface, and therefore "deeper," more personal and individual (and for that reason more universal as well, as we will later see).

Here, then, is the deep, inner experience which stands behind his sense of calling and his sense of mission, his sense of authority and the authority that others were able to see in him. It is this experience which stands behind his independence, his new vision of God and of all the people of God. It is this experience which stands behind the love he offered and was able to impart to others. Here is the depth of experience which stands behind his teaching of the love and mercy of God and behind all of his teaching, as we propose in the next chapter.

Chapter Three.
The Inner Context of Jesus.

And he taught them many things in parables, and in his teaching he said to them: 'Listen! A sower went out to sow. And as he sowed, some seed fell along the path, and the birds came and devoured it. Other seed fell on rocky ground, where it had not much soil, and immediately it sprang up, since it had no depth of soil; and when the sun rose it was scorched, and since it had no root it withered away. Other seed fell among thorns and the thorns grew up and choked it, and it yielded no grain. And other seeds fell into good soil and brought forth grain, growing up and increasing and yielding thirtyfold and sixtyfold and a hundredfold.' (Mark 4:2-8).

And he said to them, 'Is a lamp brought in to be put under a bushel, or under a bed, and not on a stand? For there is nothing hid, except to be made manifest; nor is anything secret, except to come to light.' (Mark 4:21-22).

'You fools! Did not he who made the outside make the inside also?' (Luke 11:40).

Depth in the Style of Jesus' Teaching.

Recently, Jesus' teaching has been taken note of for its stylishness and distinctiveness. And indeed he did teach in a very concise, unbelabored, highly creative way. Some of the techniques he used are mentally pleasing, as for instance parallelism (which is characteristic of much ancient Hebrew poetry), irony, and surprise instead of the expected meaning of a story. In addition, he seems to have been well-versed in hyperbole or exaggeration. His breadth of vision allowed him to take a seemingly ordinary situation, particularly in regard to human relationships, to its logical and patently pointed conclusion.

But beyond the question of the style Jesus used in teaching, there is the more significant question of where his teaching all points. What is the essence of what he was trying to say or to suggest by his teaching? To what use did he put this skill in teaching?

Even the form of Jesus' distinctive teaching style suggests the use for which it was intended. Thus, for instance, his sayings or aphorisms bespeak depth, as if they came from depth and were meant to return there (taking the listener along). Paradox in teaching which holds logical opposites in tension, and the use of images of hiddenness and interiority, suggest a kind of "instruction" which is more than the impartation of factual matter.

Jesus' most original teaching form, the parable, asserts by its nature that it is intended for depth. Stories such as the ones Jesus told are to be taken away and remembered, not for any obvious moral in them, but because their meaning is often so different from what is expected that it takes time, reflection, repetition, and increased depth to actually understand them.

These outwardly simple stories place their somewhat simple characters in familiar but morally complex and confusing situations. The morals of these stories, or that which the hearer is to take away or to glean from them, often veer sharply away from the tried and the true. Jesus is presenting, through the use of these stories and images, new ways of thinking about and seeing the world.

The parables of Jesus are simple, and yet not so simple. They have been likened by many Bible Scholars to the koans or riddles of

Zen Buddhism for their tendency to engage their hearers in a logical, in Jesus' case moral, contradiction from which there is no conceptual escape. That is, they present us often with a moral and conceptual impasse, which can open us to an entirely new and different way of thinking. Or is it a new mind with which they present us? Nonetheless, whether they present us with a new mind or a new mindset, Jesus' parables have the capacity to present us with more than we have yet received from them.

The parables were once considered allegories, often extended ones, in many cases centered around Jesus and his Lordship. But it is now thought by many scholars that the parables originally made no reference to the life of Jesus in particular but rather to the life hidden within us all, possibly to some sort of universal experience, common to all (at least in potential). Again, Jesus did not proclaim himself, at least not exclusively; he proclaimed an effectiveness we all can share.

The Parable of the Good Samaritan (Luke 10:29-37), then, is a universal story of forgiveness, showing as it does the true, personal, human nature of a class of people (Samaritans) who were considered by Jesus' audience to have been religious enemies and outcasts. This parable seems targeted to those who felt entrenched animosity toward the Samaritans as a group. Crossan (1977, 66) has pointed out that this moral boundary-crossing, telling his audience that those whom they thought were bad were actually good, produced the parable's mind-bending, "world-shattering" quality. But the depth of the story, that which has the capacity to uproot entrenched prejudices, is the universal feeling of inclusiveness which lies behind it.

The themes of Jesus' parables often deal with the process of finding or realizing something, rather than with that which is found or realized. In his parables, that which is found or realized is often spoken of as the kingdom of God, but it is portrayed in so many different images—a lost sheep, a lost coin, a prodigal son, treasure hidden in a field, a pearl of great value, a small seed which grows big, hidden leaven which causes bread dough to rise—that we have no definite conception of what exactly he was referring to. He tells us about the process of finding, that it is joyous, for instance, or effortless, but he does not explain exactly what it is that will be found except in images. That is because what he is referring to exists beyond conceptual explanation. Only our own depth, once found, can give us an indication of what it actually is.

A Different Logic.

Jesus used many tools to communicate the kingdom to others, but conceptual logic often seems to take a back seat to imagery in his teaching. Imagery works on a subconscious level, where concepts are not as neatly organized as they are in our conscious minds, and where concepts are free to take on a more open-ended form not unlike that of feelings. Such images are not usually consciously chosen in order to reinforce concepts one already holds. An image or symbol that has the capacity to resonate with others must already have been *within* in some sense, and therefore is not consciously chosen, but rather volunteers itself. Such an image has the capacity to gain the upper hand; it cannot be controlled but it can be opened, or allowed to present itself, for an image or a symbol belongs to the depth from which it comes.

Jesus spoke often about our having lost something, and our need to get it back or to get back to it. He spoke of Lost Coins and Lost Sheep and Lost Sons (all in Luke 15). He spoke of the need to grow and the need to develop (which provides our strongest clue as to his own development), as in the Yeast which expands the dough and the Mustard Seed which takes over the garden (both in Matt. 13). Yet he also spoke about the effortlessness of this growth or development, as in the Ear of Corn which grows of itself (Mark 4:26-29), while the farmer sleeps.

How had Jesus come upon these images? What is it that he wished to relate, to convey, to teach by way of these images? We will discuss the kingdom of God itself, the subject of most of Jesus' parables, in the next chapter. At the moment we are attempting to see how the images of process used by Jesus convey a depth, and an emphasis upon depth, which is rarely commented on in regard to Jesus.

Images are not strong conveyers of conceptual information. Their strength lies rather in their capacity to sink in and to remain in the mind, where at times they can reorganize its concepts, and transform its beliefs and even its feelings. Depth, once found, is full of surprises, particularly if we have spent our lives trudging across the surface.

Though it seems that Jesus' followers became concerned with creating their own society and with fitting into the larger society, Jesus himself did not focus on society, nor on any institution. When he told his followers to go out into society, if he did, he directed their focus to the individual, where the type of transformation he knew well occurs. Actually his focus was not so much *on* the individual as *within* the individual, for he had shifted the focus of salvation from following an external law to deciding upon one's inner motivation, thought and feeling. Hence his need for images and analogies in speaking about such internal matters.

The people of Jesus' time and before his time had depth, even though they had no depth psychology. They had depth, but they did not have as many ways of conceptualizing it as we do. They spoke of it in images. Even today we have few apt words with which to speak about our inner depth. How can we conceptualize an inner experience which has little meaning to those who have yet to realize it?

We will not attempt to apply any modern system of depth psychology to Jesus or to his teaching, although discoveries made beneath the surface have their analogues wherever you look. But we will insist that Jesus and his teaching cannot be understood without reference of some sort to depth, to the depth of the inner person.

The depth from which Jesus spoke and lived is something that we do not know consciously (yet) or conceptually, but it is something that we can get a feel for or come to experience, at which point it will be understood. Concepts link up with other concepts, but it takes more than concepts to see the interconnection between Jesus' teaching and ourselves. Depth is more concerned with a linkage at the level of heart.

It is not that Jesus was not logical; on the contrary, he was highly logical. But his logic was of a different type, it came from a different place, and it certainly was derived from different premises, than that conceptual, Aristotelian logic to which we are accustomed.

Some experiences say more than any words about them ever can. Our world is made up primarily of words and the concepts behind them. The words we use tend to become the reality by which we live. If words and their referents become our reality, then they can keep us pointed outward, away from our inner selves, estranged from inner reality.

Some experiences have the power to break through the self-contained reality words and concepts have produced. Once the word becomes not the reality, nor even its label, but the door to something more, then we are closer to the place where an underlying depth can at any time unfold.

Beliefs versus Belief.

In order to explain the difference between a conceptual theological issue, for example, and a nonconceptual (or not entirely conceptual) one, let us look at the issue of the existence of God. The conceptual mind, that which most of us have been following, asks whether God exists, but it has already presupposed who 'God' is, and what existence is, and it seeks to link these two concepts together. The deeper, or more-than-conceptual, mind asks the question differently, less from thought (or curiosity) alone, and less to uphold its already existing beliefs, and more from inner longing, a yearning will-to-know, and from inner experience. As John A. T. Robinson (1963, 55, italics his) has stated, "The question of God is the question *whether this depth of being is a reality or an illusion*, not whether *a* Being exists beyond the bright blue sky, or anywhere else."

Which question is the more significant? Which has the power to affect the reality of the person who asks it? Therefore, which of these questions comes from depth?

It does not really matter whether or not God exists according to our former conceptions if belief is more than conceptual. Binding definitions have hitched beliefs to concepts, so that now we say "beliefs" rather than "belief." "Beliefs" may be quasi-logical propositions, but they are based on premises whose certainty remains in our feeling and in our subjective experience. In any case, we believe first, rationalize later. "Belief," as in the initial sense of trust, prior to any logical conception of it, is closer to the true origin of faith.

We believe not because we understand the logic behind Jesus' sayings, not because his logic in every way agrees with our own, but because we don't understand and because his logic comes from a place that we want deeply to go. We believe because the foundations of our house, our world and ourselves, have been shifted, and because our only other options are to ignore it or to actively deny it. The real belief is the underlying trust which does not and cannot depend on concepts. As we plunge farther and farther into the depth of this trust, which is also the depth of ourselves, then logic comes; it pieces itself together, without our "help" and without our control.

Another basic difference is that beliefs tend to "know," and therefore cannot accommodate new or different information as it comes in, whereas belief, which does not yet know, has the capacity to use whatever it can find. Jesus had belief: he had faith and trust in God and, through this trust in God, he was able to trust his own deeper experience. We, on the other hand, have beliefs, which are stored among the other concepts in our minds, and so we cannot draw upon them for anything much deeper than argument and contention. What good would a logical conviction of salvation be if it had no depth behind it, and no depth of heart within it?

Jesus loses those who seek to hear his words with logic, if their logic is based primarily on premises and assumptions they learned in the past before they heard him. For Jesus presents us with his own context, entirely different from the world and the mind to which we have become accustomed. In order to understand his words, it is necessary to step out of our own context and to enter his.

Jesus loses those who seek to retain their former way of seeing the world, others, God, or themselves. He loses those who seek to retain their former system of conceptual understanding. To believe in Jesus, and in what he presents us with, is to begin to join him in freeing our minds from the domination of man-made systems and even natural laws.

Jesus' words come from a place far removed from the place in which we contain conceptual logic. So does our belief, our faith, our trust. Our belief comes from within us, certainly, but not from anything with which we are yet well-acquainted. It is not pieced together by our interlocking of concepts; it does not come from words; it does not even come from ourselves.

To ask what it means to believe is to deepen belief and therefore to strengthen it considerably, because simply to ask is to prepare oneself to accept a reply which comes from beyond the intellect. If we do not allow the response to come of itself, then it is likely that we ourselves will choose a reply which is grounded in little more than the intellect, which, depending on the premises it has already accepted, may not run very deep at all, and therefore may prove a very shaky foundation for something so central to many lives.

The basis of belief is not fear in any form; belief comes neither from fear of death, nor from anxiety about what will happen after death. Belief comes from a more present concern, and therefore, at the moment in which it is felt, a more pressing concern: How can we come to a realization of a deeper and altogether different form of reality here in our earthly lives? The question almost presumes that we have a certain capacity that we are not putting to proper—perhaps to any—use.

Holy Puzzlement.

The human mind wants and craves answers. It wants to know. But it must work under limited and limiting conditions to know everything that it wants to know. Yet we want or need to know so badly that before we really know, before all the facts are in, we tend to believe that we already know.

Perhaps that is because there is a discomfort inherent in not-knowing. Yet this admission (of not knowing), uncomfortable as it may be, is the first step in attaining knowledge of life and the realization of life itself.

"Ask, and it will be given you; seek, and you will find; knock, and it will be opened to you" (Matthew 7:7). These words suggest the necessary attitude for the acquisition of that which Jesus taught. This attitude might be symbolized as "lostness" or even as sacred confusion in that it would seem to be a kind of temporary bewilderment, a temporary admission (to oneself) that one does not know. It is an attitude of seeking without knowing what you are looking for, of asking without knowing what the answer is, and of knocking without knowing at whose doorstep you stand.

We leave our own personal will at the door when we knock. To ask is to open oneself for a response which comes from beyond oneself. For though we may have the concept down cold, and we may have the beliefs rolling off our tongue, we are still a long way from knowledge, a long way from experience, and a long way from certainty.

Therefore it is emptiness that Jesus asks of his followers. This is not only an emptiness of hands, of pockets or purses, for which he asks; it is emptiness of mental tinkering, emptiness of judgment, and even emptiness of beliefs in order to be filled with belief itself. It is an emptiness of concepts and surface thought, so that depth might arise.

We don't know what the world is, although we think we do. We don't know what God is either. And we don't even know ourselves. Once we have realized this, then we will know what emptiness is, and just how little knowledge and even salvation require of us.

All we have is a *sense* of salvation; we may have derived this from Jesus himself. We sense it in him but we do not know what it is, and we do not know how to realize it or make it real. We depend on him, his depth and knowledge, to show us the way to our own.

Even the most intent of Jesus' listeners were led into a state of temporary puzzlement by him. Jesus challenged their expectations just enough to create in them this state of emptiness and unknowing. Jesus caused them to doubt their former perceptions of the world and to believe instead in what he and—through him and through themselves—what depth itself told them and showed them.

Depth and knowledge appear on their own accord, as if by their own will. Jesus himself comes to those who are lost.

Interconnection.

What specifically is the depth behind Jesus' ideas and words, and the depth behind his life? Nearly all of his ideas suggest an underlying interconnection within the human being, among human beings, and between human beings and God. The measure that you put in is the measure you get back (Mark 4:24); you are forgiven as you forgive (Matt. 6:14). Such interconnection is the essence of his teaching, and, according to his teaching, such interconnection is the essence of life.

Interconnection, in the form of interrelationship, the relationship between and among individuals, is present in every one of Jesus' parables. Even the mustard plant becomes a home and a haven for birds and for other living creatures; as it grows, it grows in relation to the life which exists all around it and, now, within it (Mark 4:30-32). However, it is primarily within the human relationships offered by Jesus as examples that we recognize the great correspondence between daily life and a higher reality. For Jesus offers for our consideration relationships with overtones of sly ingenuity (the dishonest steward, in Luke 16:1-7), relationships grounded in envy and jealousy (the vineyard laborers, in Matt. 20:1-13), relationships hinging on romantic love and longing (bridesmaids and bridegroom, as in Matt. 25:1-13), relationships which depend on persistent asking (the bothersome widow and unrighteous judge, in Luke 18:1-5), relationships shaded by greed and distrust (the wicked tenants, in Luke 20:9-19), relationships established on the impulse of pulling people in from the streets for a spur-of-the-moment banquet (Gos. Thom. Log. 64/Luke 14:16-24). All of this seems to say that even those relationships which would seem to have the least connection with God, or with religion in general, have, when seen with depth, a great correspondence.

As he uses relationships of all kinds to convey his message, Jesus deepens such relationships so that they begin to have more significance than they would seem to have from a surface viewpoint. A business relationship, for instance, is no longer simply a business relationship; in some way, even some offbeat way, it symbolizes our relationship to God. Every relationship we have here on earth has some bearing upon, some significance regarding, ourselves and therefore our relationship to God. That which we are bound to on earth has the potential to loosen our staid thinking and to lift us to heaven.

We look out at the very same world (in effect), but we cannot see what he had seen. We cannot see God in the ravens and in the lilies; we cannot see Him in those of whom we feel jealous or mistrustful. We cannot see the connection between all things and God because we cannot see the connection between God and ourselves. Our constructs are too weak, too shaky, and too limited by what we think we already know to tell us about such interconnection.

We cannot ordinarily see this interconnection, and that is why it must be taught to us, or why it must come to us, as apparently it had come to Jesus. Jesus states that it does not come to us because we are not looking for it. We need to seek it out because we do not know what it is. If we go out looking for it, but believe we already know conceptually what we are looking for, then how will we be open to it when it really comes?

Jesus' life shows the same interconnection as his teaching. For though he was independent, though he was an authority, though he had come to be selfless, he seemed at one with those who were dependent, some dependent on authority, some dependent on self. Though he has come to be considered holy, and perfect in every way, he seemed during his lifetime to have been most at home with those who were considered sinners under religious law and the purity system, at home with those who were imperfect and estranged in some way, perhaps in many ways. Jesus saw within these people the same perfection that we see in him, and he healed them with it. He sat and he spoke with these so-called sinners, and he communed with them and he communicated with them. He found within them an interconnection with something that he had felt and experienced within himself, an interconnection which ran deeper than their shared estrangement; it was something that joined them together, something he lived by and taught them to live by.

At the deepest level, according to one with self-knowledge, the individual is one. Heart and mind and soul and strength come together and reveal to us the true nature of ourselves. Paradoxically, it is at the moment when we come to self-knowledge that we come upon knowledge of others, and both of these together provide us with at least the beginnings of the knowledge of God. When we come to a realization of our deepest longing—i.e., for whatever it is that we have lost or are lost from and need to get back to—then we will have found ourselves and, at the same time, we will have found the kingdom of God as well.

Jesus sought the participation of others (by extension, that includes ourselves) in an inner reality: his own inner reality. To enter his reality is to enter the kingdom. It is to hear his words and to do them. It is to believe in him.

The words of Jesus take time, study, and meditation to understand because they must be heard with the depth with which they were originally spoken. It takes time to acquire such depth, often, as well as intensive effort, after which time and effort there must also be a letting-go, or an effortlessness, for in reality this depth comes only of its own accord.

Chapter Four.
The Kingdom of God.

And he said, 'With what can we compare the kingdom of God, or what parable shall we use for it? It is like a grain of mustard seed, which, when sown upon the ground, is the smallest of all the seeds on earth; yet when it is sown it grows up and becomes the greatest of all shrubs, and puts forth large branches, so that the birds of the air can make nests in its shade.' (Mark 4:30-32).

'The kingdom of heaven is like treasure hidden in a field, which a man found and covered up; then in his joy he goes and sells all that he has and buys that field.' (Matthew 13:44).

'Again, the kingdom of heaven is like a merchant in search of fine pearls, who, on finding one pearl of great value, went and sold all that he had and bought it.' (Matthew 13:45-46).

To Enter the Kingdom.

Reading his words, we are struck by the many different ways in which Jesus tried to describe the kingdom of God. Not only did he express it in images, sayings, and parables, but he expressed it in various types of images, in various types of sayings, and in various types of parables. The kingdom of God is, according to the Synoptic Gospels of Mark, Matthew, and Luke, at the heart of Jesus' teaching (whereas John employs instead the telling phrase "eternal life"). And yet, because Jesus spoke about it in so many different ways, it may be difficult to get a clear conceptual understanding of what the kingdom of God means.

"'Truly, I say to you, whoever does not receive the kingdom of God like a child shall not enter it'" (Luke 18:17). "'Whoever humbles himself like this child, he is the greatest in the kingdom of heaven'" (Matt. 18:4). This is Jesus reversing the way of the world. In the world, the important things are those things we strive for and become, while in Jesus' view, the important things are those things we already have within us yet rarely let out. The kingdom is not something to be conceptualized; that is not how it is learned, received, entered, or let grow. Children generally bypass conceptualization for action; they jump in with both feet, learning by experimentation, trial and error, rather than by design.

Jesus' sayings and parables about the kingdom are less seeds of instruction than they are seeds of experience. His images refer to something deeper than mental constructs (or other words); they refer to deeper referents that cannot be comprehended with a surface hearing. It is only increased openness which can hear them—the openness of a child for instance, or the openness of a lost person whose only hope is to be found by God.

The kingdom of God is more than a construct because it happens to be alive. It is a living thing, just as we ourselves are living things, though it has no body, no individual personality, and no dependence upon the earth for its being. The kingdom is a form of life with which we are not now familiar.

The kingdom of God is an idea, but it is more than a rational construct. Some ideas have a life of their own. The kingdom is an idea which cannot be thought about from the outside; it must be entered into and/or released to be fully known. Some ideas require that we forego the usual dissociation of ourselves from what we are learning, if we are to learn at all. Some learning requires participation, and participation of the whole being, not only the intellect; it requires first-hand experience. Some learning cannot help but to circle back around and include ourselves within it.

The kingdom is hidden, like most other ideas, until it grows, at which point it can be seen anywhere. If we have an idea in mind, and keep it in mind, then that idea will soon spring up everywhere we look. And, because the kingdom gathers together "fish of every kind" (Matt. 13:47)—both people and ideas of every kind—the kingdom *is* everywhere, once it is seen at all.

But first the kingdom must be found, and to be found it must be sought. But how can we seek it if we have no idea what it means, and no idea what an idea is (for that matter)? How do we look for or land upon an idea which is not merely a construct, which we cannot simply memorize and/or recall from personal memory?

Luckily, the kingdom has a mind of its own, and it will meet us when we are ready for it. Like other ideas which we keep in our minds—ideas which compel us (from afar) until we take them in and allow them to impel us (from within), ideas which reinforce themselves whenever we share them with others (ACIM), ideas which motivate us and provide us with a passion we did not know we had—the kingdom can be gradually entered into as we allow it to enter us. This would entail simply trying to see it as it is, and then taking whatever we understand of it into ourselves, allowing it to teach us from within, learning more about its reality, and then taking in more and more of it, until we have it entered fully.

Before we would decide for such an alternative life and reality, we would have to learn as much as we can about it. And our learning about it begins with our growing conviction that the living kingdom exists within us, as an inner reality—whether psychological or spiritual or both. And, toward this conviction that the kingdom of God exists inside us, let us see what Jesus himself taught about this.

The Kingdom is Within You.

What does it mean that Jesus tried to express the kingdom of God in so many different ways, using so many different images? It suggests to us that the kingdom is hard to describe, that it is intangible, an inner reality, a reality that must be willed before it can be perceived, something related to the depth we have been told exists within us.

And this Jesus states directly as well:

> Being asked by the Pharisees when the kingdom of God was coming, he answered them, 'The kingdom of God is not coming with signs to be observed; nor will they say, "Lo, here it is!" or "There!" for behold, the kingdom of God is within you' (Luke 17:20-21).

Can a teacher be any more direct than this? Even the context supports the translation of the phrase, *entos hymon* (Frye, 54), "The kingdom of God is *within you.*" For it "is not coming with signs to be observed." "Nor will they say, 'Lo, here it is!' or 'There!'" The kingdom is not an external, but rather an internal, reality, until we have learned to see from it, at which point it is both.

Some ideas are objective realities; they are not ours alone because they were not thought up as constructs. In a sense, such ideas realize themselves, without our doing much, if anything, to help them. Perhaps they come from some sort of more-than-personal part of ourselves we are not generally aware of, perhaps from what Carl Jung called the "collective unconscious." In any case, the place from which these ideas come belongs to no one individual, not even to Jesus, according to John 12:49: "'For I have not spoken on my own authority; the Father who sent me has himself given me commandment what to say and what to speak.'"

The kingdom grows effortlessly, as a reality unto itself. This is the gist of Mark 4:26-28:

'The kingdom of God is as if a man should scatter
  seed upon the ground,
and should sleep and rise night and day,
and the seed should sprout and grow,
he knows not how.
The earth produces of itself,
first the blade,
then the ear,
then the full grain in the ear.'

This is an analogy for an inner state of unfoldment, for a process which is both psychological and spiritual. We "sleep" while the process unfolds; we are not conscious of its growth, in the sense that we do not direct it. It has a mind of its own, and it is larger, perhaps more all-encompassing than our personal selves, like the earth in relation to individuals, like the sun in relation to its satellites.

Supporting evidence for seeing Jesus' idea of the kingdom of God as an inner reality can be found in Jesus' continual emphasis on the inner state of the person rather than upon his or her behavior (as in Luke 11:37-41, which speaks of cleaning the inside of the cup as well as the outside). Though psychology as a science did not yet exist, Jesus and the early Christians were certainly able to distinguish between the outside and the inside of a person.

Only something which is internal and yet not constructed could be spoken of in the wide variety of metaphor Jesus used to speak about the kingdom. If the kingdom were an idea, an experience, a feeling, or a new way of thinking about or perceiving the world, then we could enter it, receive it, refuse (to accept) it, realize it (within ourselves), notice that it unfolds without our conscious effort, and grow convinced that it holds a value which is not of this world.

And what else could be spoken of as *both* present and future, as the kingdom is, except something internal which can be realized now or put off until later? The kingdom as an idea or inner reality is always present; if it is not present for you now, then it must be future.

The Negative Side of Within.

What is behind the persona, the part of ourselves that we show the world and admit to ourselves? We know that at one level deeper than the surface there exist pride and want, and fierce competitiveness born of apparent desperation. Each of us has felt the ever-evaporating fullness of self. But behind the constructed self, what is there? We do not know because we fear our inner reality. We particularly fear a part of our inner reality, or rather a distortion of our reality, which some psychologists call our "shadow."

We fear that at heart we are really monsters, that our true inner reality is evil and/or reckless and wild and that it needs to be kept firmly in check (ACIM). We live daily with this fear, but we have adjusted to it and in fact have built an entire civilization over top of it. We have successfully restrained it but have never quite confined it. As much as we have tried, we have never quite forgotten the dark part of ourselves. Though all might appear well and orderly on the surface, each of us has the sense that something powerful and ugly is brewing underneath, but we are afraid to find out exactly what it is.

We are afraid even to think about it, afraid to look in its direction let alone to confront it. We don't even want to admit to ourselves the possibility that anything more exists within us than what we can see on the surface. We don't want to admit the possibility that things are not exactly what they seem to be. And yet such fear comes over us whenever we even think of looking inside ourselves.

The longer we refuse to acknowledge the inner part of ourselves, the less we will know about it, and the more afraid we will be to acknowledge it. Our vivid imaginations present us with concepts and images of what it might be like, and, because we have little firm or first-hand information to go on, we tend to believe these vivid images based on fear.

What is the true nature of the shadow side of ourselves, the outer layer of our inner world which scares us off and stands as a barrier to the rest? We can get a glimpse of the shadow as it emerges from time to time in our everyday lives. Whenever we are upset for no real reason, that is the shadow pulling free from our restraints. Whenever darkness and gloom creep over our day, that is the shadow coming over us, assuming control. Whenever we are spiteful or resentful or vengeful, even self-righteously so, even when we "know" we are in the right and the other must be wrong, that is the shadow manifesting the fruit of its constant effort to wrest control.

The shadow does not give up; it will not cede as long as we remain on its level, as long as we keep our minds trained upon the surface. It entices us with pride, the pride of self-generation, as if we ourselves made ourselves and can therefore control everything in our domain, and then it pulls back so that we forget it is there. Only at times does this pride of the surface reveal its true colors: behind it stand self-abasement, self-hatred, and guilt.

What do we feel guilty about? What, if anything, have we done (or failed to do) which we feel guilty about?

We have limited ourselves, and then placed all of our trust in limitation. We trust more in that which we have made than in that which is given us. We have forsaken who we really are, underneath all else. On an unconscious level, this misplaced trust, this forsaking of the truth of ourselves, is guilt-inducing. We have become rich in self, and proud of our apparent independence from God and from other people. Yet beneath the surface, what do we have for our independence from others except estrangement and fear—fear of others, fear of God, fear even of our deeper selves?

The shadow, immersed in self-devaluation, forsaking our true value, presses us to exert effort to become something other than what we are. A vicious circle ensues. First we try to compensate for our negative self-image by thinking ourselves great, but the real basis of such compensation only reinforces the negative and debased self-image. That which we are trying to compensate for becomes stronger, and therefore we must compensate all the more, with the result that, soon, the image of ourselves we try to keep in mind becomes grandiose and delusional, while on the other hand the image we keep trying to suppress seems utterly debased. That is, we think too highly of the surface of ourselves, and too lowly of that which lurks within. Thus do the peaks of the surface, upon reflection, point directly to the valleys just below.

Our task, then, in religious and psychological terms, is to "confront the person within us for whom the Law is necessary" (Sanford, 35). This does not mean that we challenge this part of ourselves, or fight against it in any way. That is what we have been doing, perpetually (because it hasn't worked), when we have not been hiding it or projecting it onto someone else (ACIM). We need instead to recognize it for what it is, which is a distortion, part of the overall false image we have made of ourselves (ACIM). And then we need to go deeper still, and find what is beyond the shadow, for only light can cast a shadow. We need to go deeper still in order to find our true selves.

The Kingdom is also Within You.

Though the poison is within the human heart, so is the antidote, the solution. That Jesus apparently believed this to be so points up his tremendous trust of the human heart. We talk about our faith in him, and his faith in God: what about his faith in us? He trusted the heart of the sinner enough to commune with that person, so that the sinner no longer stood apart, and therefore was sinner no longer. He trusted the heart of the sick person enough to join with him or her in faith, until the sickness no longer set them apart, and so the person was healed of sickness. And he trusted his own heart, somehow, enough to allow it to distinguish between appearance and reality.

The shadow is not our depth, not our reality. How could it possibly be our depth if it is not whole, having no reality in and of itself? The shadow, which often manifests itself as a reaction to the surface, lies only a bit below the surface. But it is no different from who we think we are upon the surface in that it has no more reality than the surface image we project.

There are many thoughts and feelings which seem to be internal, but which are really only another layer of the surface. They can be discerned by noticing their objects: what they focus upon, or harken back to. "Thus you will know them by their fruits" (Matt. 7:20). For they arise from the very surface to which they point back.

What Jesus found below the surface, behind even the shadow, is what he seeks to present to us, to explain to us in whatever way he can, through whatever images he can use. What he found below the surface, behind even the shadow, is the kingdom of God. It is a firmer foundation than that upon which we had been basing our lives because it is given; it is not self-generated. It is there. It is real in and of itself, an objective reality (though it is within). It stands alone, but it ensures that we ourselves never need to.

The process itself of finding is interesting because inherent in it is the suggestion that what is to be found is something that we once had. In the Parable of the Lost Sheep (Matt. 18:12-13 and Luke 15:4-6) and the Parable of the Lost Coin (Luke 15:8-9) this is certainly true. It is also true in the Parable of the Prodigal Son (Luke 15:11-32), in which story the father exclaims that his son "was lost, and is found" (v. 24).

And then there are the parables which speak of that which is found as something which is stumbled upon, but recognized to be of great value. These parables include those of the Treasure in the Field (Matt. 13:44) and the Pearl of Great Price (Matt. 13:45-46). In both of these parables, the kingdom is likened to a reality that had been buried, concealed from our sight, but which is now made manifest.

Such hiddenness of something now made manifest is also the process found in the parables of the Mustard Seed (Mark 4:30-32) and the Leaven (or yeast) hidden in bread, causing it to rise (Matt. 13:33; Luke 13:20-21). Such parables tell us that the kingdom grows stronger and more powerful in us once we see past the shadow which had hidden it and impeded its growth. As it grows, it branches out through your relationships and grows out into the world. One gets the sense that the nature of the kingdom is always to grow, always to increase (ACIM), always to interconnect.

What is it that we have lost, but that we stumble upon and find to be of inestimable value? Could it be as simple as our sense that God cares for us and that we, more than anything, care for Him and for one another? Could our loss of this sense have been the reason we had not trusted Him to lead us and to help us, and the reason we felt we had to depend upon our own efforts to achieve His grace?

Once, it had been hidden from our eyes. We could see only the world, only the surface, and what the surface could see. The surface was all we wanted to see because we feared that which was within ourselves. Even our shadow, that which we feared was utterly negative within us, was a product of surface concerns. We had not trusted ourselves (or our Creator) enough to go within and past our fear.

Yet why do we fear whatever might exist beyond the limited range of our physical senses? Why do we trust our physical senses so willingly? Is it simply because we have made ourselves familiar with them? Or is it because we fear what they cannot show?

Once we have found the kingdom, however, just below our fear, we realize that our fears were unfounded. Our fears had no bearing on the reality within us. It was only because it was hidden that we did not recognize what was truly within us, nor leap for joy that it was there. It was only because we had forgotten who we really are that we must find it again.

Sanford (27) cites Fritz Kunkel's having noted that in the parable in Matthew 13:45-46, it is the kingdom itself which is seeking the pearls of great value, which indicates that "*we* are the pearls, the treasure found by the kingdom of God." The kingdom comes with its own will, and we ourselves are inherent within that will.

Jesus says about those who enter the kingdom: "'I tell you, among those born of women none is greater than John; yet he who is least in the kingdom of God is greater than he'" (Luke 7:28). That is, the mere presence of the kingdom automatically makes us more, and more valuable, than we have thought ourselves to have been. Obviously, then, in Jesus' way of seeing, our value does not depend on what we have thought of ourselves in the past.

The kingdom of God is larger, broader, and more inclusive than the selves we've made, yet it is within ourselves. It provides us with a new self, one that is more than a construct. The kingdom of God is at once who we really are and where we really exist. It is our true home.

Chapter Five.
Forgiveness.

'But I say to you that hear, Love your enemies, do good to those who hate you, bless those who curse you, pray for those who abuse you. To him who strikes you on the cheek, offer the other also; and from him who takes away your coat do not withhold even your shirt. Give to everyone who begs from you; and of him who takes away your goods do not ask them again. And as you wish that men would do to you, do so to them.' (Luke 6:27-31).

Then Peter came up and said to him, 'Lord, how often shall my brother sin against me, and I forgive him? As many as seven times?' Jesus said to him, 'I do not say to you seven times, but seventy times seven.' (Matt. 18:21-22).

'Therefore I tell you, her sins … are forgiven, for she loved much; but he who is forgiven little, loves little.' (Luke 7:47).

The Needlessness of Judgment.

One does not forgive in order to feel morally righteous. Though morality is often taken to be the essence of Christianity, Jesus' religion was not based on morality or upon a sense of moral righteousness. His teaching on forgiveness shows this, for, in saying, "'But if anyone strikes you on the right cheek, turn to him the other also'" (Matt. 5:39), Jesus is, in Crossan's words, "no longer giving helpful moral admonition or even radical pacifistic advice." Rather, Jesus is here "deliberately overthrowing ethics" (1973, 82).

Jesus turned the other cheek not because he was a martyr but because he had a sense (perhaps to the level of certainty) of what was truly significant. He taught his followers to forgive so that they might land upon the same sense of significance.

Religion needs a more-than-moral standard, a more-than-moral certainty, and, for that matter, a more-than-conceptual certainty. Jesus took morality itself to a deeper foundation than that of rules to follow. He told anyone who would listen that it is by getting one's thinking right, and then one's feeling, that one's behavior will right itself. Morality, in essence, begins in the heart and deeper mind; from there, behavior follows.

Had Jesus instead thought, as so many of us do, 'What rule have I to follow, what act have I to perform, to come under the grace and mercy of God?,' then he would not have been Jesus. His message is clear, but it is rarely clearly heard: There is no rule that one can follow, no act one can perform, to get oneself under the grace and mercy of God. God's grace and mercy are freely given; they are unconditional. They are felt, or experienced, by a transformed mind.

Jesus did not wait for "sinners" to change their lives; he went out and met them where they were. It was his mere presence among them which changed them, if necessary. It was the fact that he did not judge them which enabled them to stop judging themselves. It was his introduction of the love of God into their lives which transformed their minds.

A society needs rules in order to run effectively, but God is different. Just as the things of Caesar are not God's (Mark 12:17), neither are the ways of Caesar God's ways. We tend to associate, and to confuse, the authority we can see with the God we cannot see. There are clearer ways to sense and to see God in the world, and ways that are more in line with Jesus' teaching. God can be felt and sensed, seen and experienced within a person, where His kingdom has been established, within oneself and within every one of our earthly relationships. As C. H. Dodd (68) states:

> It is in this field of human relations, where the issues are most acute and the emotions are most strongly aroused, that the absoluteness of God's requirements can be exposed. This is part of what is meant by the declaration that his kingdom is here.

If we wait instead for Him and His kingdom to show up on earth by way of our world's authorities and institutions (of any kind), then we will probably be waiting an awfully long time.

Jesus' ideas continue to bring a sense of forgiveness into the world which undermines our former sense of the world, and our former sense of identity, and even our former sense of God. Jesus gave freely of his own sense of the overwhelming love and power of God. Once this has been felt, in the direct and simple sense in which Jesus expressed it in Matthew's Sermon on the Mount (Chapters 5 through 7) and Luke's Sermon on the Plain (6:17-6:49), then no thought of condemnation or judgment can withstand it. No cry of vengeance or retribution can be heard within it.

One does not forgive in order to see oneself as better than another person. Nor does one forgive in order to be morally right, or righteous. What good is moral certitude in the face of an injustice which cries out for revenge and retribution? Rather, one forgives specifically to overcome all thought of retribution, all thought of vengeance, and all thought of moral certainty or moral righteousness. One forgives in order to allow one's mind to be transformed.

God's Forgiveness and Our Own.

What is the benefit that the forgiver derives from forgiveness? From our current standpoint, it would seem that there is no benefit to the forgiver; yet the one we forgive has the benefit of being able to walk away scot-free. From our current way of thinking, the one who is forgiven derives everything, while the one who forgives derives nothing. Who would consent to forgive under such an arrangement?

There must be a modicum of self-interest inherent in forgiveness or no one would consent to it. If it does not make one morally righteous, then what could the benefit of forgiveness be?

Forgiveness does not make one morally perfect, but it does convey a certain sense of perfection, a certain wholeness, which bestows a certain sharing of the character of God. According to the Sermons (Matt. 5:43-48; Luke 6:27-36), complete forgiveness shares God's character perfectly, and makes us the Children of God. This goes beyond all sense of morality and all sense of conception. It is a felt certainty, an experienced perfection. Joachim Jeremias (29) noted that Jesus responded to any censure by his critics by indicating that he was simply following who he knew God to be, saying, in effect, "So kind, so full of compassion for the poor—are you going to censure him?"

Another reason that it would help us to learn to forgive is that our judgment of others haunts ourselves. Here is another reason Jesus associated our forgiveness of others with the forgiveness of God (as in Matt. 6:14). If we do not forgive, we will not realize the forgiveness that has already been given freely to us, despite what we think we have done against God, either directly or through our earthly relationships.

For Jesus, God inhabited deepest conscience. That is why love could fulfill all the requirements of the law (Matt. 22:36-40). Our deepest conscience is something more than a protector of society or of the ego. The conscience is more than an arbiter of morality. In fact, conscience can often be distinguished from surface fear by the way it does not always accord with our own, conscious sense of morality.

Conscience lies deeper than the shadow, deeper than our deepest fear. Conscience is that which God has placed within us in order to allow us to discern, not so much right from wrong, as reality from illusion. (As such, conscience has been identified with the Holy Spirit, the spirit of discernment. It was this, an experience rather than a concept, that Jesus as a risen, spiritual being helped to evoke or spark in his followers.)

It is by overlooking what we thought was reality that we are led to a realization that we had misinterpreted, and mistaken illusion for reality. It is at this point of "lostness," of not knowing where else to turn for reality, that depth is evoked from within us. Depth replaces illusion with reality, a reality of an entirely different kind than the surface to which we have grown accustomed.

Our judgment of others ensures that our own guilt will continue to haunt us. One might even say that that is its underlying purpose. Judging others puts us in the arena of judgment where we fear we might be judged ourselves. Doing so keeps us from realizing the true nature of God, and of ourselves, via the resources within us, including the conscience, the Spirit, and the love He has placed in our hearts.

Guilt is forever based on something from the past. If the past is gone, but the guilt remains, then something is wrong. For it is not guilt that keeps us from doing something wrong; it is rather our inherent love of righteousness, and our inherent love, which smooths our path. Guilt is an affliction from which each of us suffers, no matter what it is we may have done or refrained from doing. Our judgment of others attempts to find something, often an arbitrary something (ACIM), in another person on which to pin this guilt which we cannot or will not deal with in ourselves, but it always returns to haunt us again. We cannot rid ourselves of our own guilt by projecting it out to others, by making enemies.

Guilt is part of the universal human condition. It need not be attached to any wrongdoing on our part, nor any sin or sinful behavior, yet it is there, and it is strong. Guilt is a free-floating condition, with no conscious object, until we find something to pin it on. Thus do we denigrate ourselves for our behavior, even if it was not harmful to anyone. For those seeking reasons to feel guilty, the world becomes like a hall of mirrors. And thus do we become impassioned about others' faults and misdeeds.

Jesus' strong emphasis on forgiveness suggests the importance he gave to dealing with this guilt. His practice of forgiving those he healed (e.g., Matt. 9:2; Luke 7:47-48) suggests that he saw guilt at the root of their sickness or estrangement. Perhaps he believed, and rather effectively so, that the problem (in whatever form) was a manifestation or expression of the (unnecessary) guilt which lay inside.

The people Jesus healed were able to look at him and see a person who stood guiltless before God. Seeing Jesus as guiltless, and seeing that he saw them as guiltless, they now had the capacity to see others this way, not excluding themselves.

The importance of forgiveness in Jesus' teaching suggests the significance of guilt in the life of the individual. Even today, guilt seems to underlie nearly all of our relations with God. "Lord, have mercy" and "Lord, I am not worthy" are familiar refrains of the worshipper. Jesus' relationship with God seems to have been based not on the guilt and fear an authoritarian God might provoke, but rather it was based on the love a compassionate father might inspire. It is our forgiveness of others which allows us to share this same sense of the love of God.

Jesus' advice to all his followers was basically not to judge at all. For he knew about the tendency of the human being to judge another more harshly for that which the one sitting in judgment has not yet dealt with in himself.

> 'Judge not, that you be not judged. For with the judgment you pronounce you will be judged, and the measure you give will be the measure you get. Why do you see the speck that is in your brother's eye, but do not notice the log that is in your own eye?' (Matt. 7:1-3)

Judgment cannot emanate from a humble cast of mind. It arises from a wish for superiority which is itself born of an underlying sense of inferiority. Why else would anyone attempt to reinforce or enhance oneself at the expense of others? Those who are truly forgiven are those who feel free to forgive. Those who *have* and have abundantly are those who feel free to include others in what they have. What they have, at base, is peace, peace enough to give, peace enough to understand forgiveness.

We try our best to fool ourselves, to convince ourselves that we judge others in order to help them, in order to bring them around to the right kind of morality (i.e., our own). But as it is practiced, judgment divides, excluding those who will not change, and creating rifts between well-intentioned sides.

We can be saved from guilt only as we find the strength in our hearts to forgive those we have already judged. Once we have found forgiveness, we will have found the grace and mercy of God. In a word, forgive these others, and you will feel the forgiveness of God.

Here again, in Jesus' teaching on forgiveness, is the idea of interconnection. In the Golden Rule: "'And as you wish that men would do to you, do so to them'" (Luke 6:31), how we treat others is how we can expect to be treated. There is interconnection among human relationships.

> 'Judge not, and you will not be judged; condemn not, and you will not be condemned; forgive, and you will be forgiven; give, and it will be given to you; good measure, pressed down, shaken together, running over, will be put into your lap. For the measure you give will be the measure you get back.' (Luke 6:37-38).

Our relationships are not isolated as we tend to think of them. Earthly relationships have universal causes and universal effects. Even personal feelings are universalized in Jesus' way of thinking.

But there is also interconnection, in Jesus' teaching, between God's forgiveness and our own. Our forgiveness of others transforms God (in our human minds) from Judge to Care-giver. When we begin to think differently about those we can see, then we can begin to think differently about Him we cannot see.

Judgment encircles and isolates mistakes. It fails to see the rest of the person, the whole of the person. The one who judges very rarely ever sees or notices how much judgment isolates not only the one who is judged but also the one who judges.

The more we distance our fellow human beings, the more distant God seems to us. We have not isolated those we have judged so much as we have isolated ourselves. Sitting in judgment, we are left alone, alone with nothing but our lonely sense of moral certainty. Willing to forgive, however, we are joined with others at a level beyond conception.

Heavenly Rewards.

Forgiveness seems to ask the impossible of us. It asks that we do things and think things and feel things that simply make no sense to the world. Forgiveness asks that we place ourselves, the selves we've grown up with, the selves we've come to identify with, in a position of secondary concern.

That is why forgiveness is understandable only to a changed mind. The premises we currently hold to do not allow for it. Therefore it is not something that Jesus asks his followers to understand; rather, forgiveness is something that he asks them to practice.

Forgiveness is the "doable" (do-able) part of Jesus' teaching, the part that prepares one to enter the more esoteric kingdom of God. It is the means of seeing, achieving, and receiving the goal and the vision of the kingdom. It is the work that we can do (or have done through us) to hasten realization of the kingdom. Forgiveness is the "act" which changes one's context, one's inner world.

That having been said, forgiveness, like belief or love, is not really an action we take. When all is said and done, forgiveness is not "doable." There is nothing for us to do in forgiveness, except to decide to forgive. It is an act of mind and of will, rather than of observable behavior. It is something that is done within one's heart, "secretly," so to speak, much like prayer, and not so much for the other person as for oneself and one's own peace of mind.

What do we do to forgive but decide to overlook a part of the surface? What do we do to forgive but decide that we will allow our minds to change? To forgive is, in effect, to ask to see the reality of depth; it is to ask for a transformation of mind. To forgive and to forgive continually is to give up all one's former beliefs, all the beliefs upon which the world is based, in order to receive another belief, a belief which is not really from ourselves at all.

Forgiveness ends the world, for each of us, for the forgiver and the forgiven, as it is applied within our worldly relationships. This world-ending aspect of forgiveness sets the stage for the effective re-creation or re-organization of the world as experienced within the kingdom of God. "'No one who puts his hand to the plow and looks back is fit for the kingdom of God'" (Luke 9:62). Forgiveness opens us to a new world and a new self by allowing us to forget the past.

What does it mean to forgive but to forget the past? Whether it is to forget some past situation, some past action, or some past intention, to forgive is to forget that which has in actuality already faded away. Therefore to forgive is also to open oneself to the real and to the reality of the present. When the present moment arrives dragging no past behind it, then the world is changed.

The world is changed when we see it differently. It is transformed when we ourselves are transformed. If our enemy is no longer our enemy, then the world has changed, and is now filled with righteousness (at least for a moment). When the past, even if only a second ago, is distinguished from the present by the very strength of the present moment, then the present is freed, and we are freed, from that which held us back. At that point the future is truly open, our perception of reality has shifted, and all things are possible.

But to attempt to retain a past identity is to bar oneself from this example of heaven and to withhold oneself from life itself. Past hurts and past judgments have a way of holding us to the past. Each of us is a gatekeeper of sorts; but in our attempt to hold others out, we hold ourselves out as well. Our attempt to remove joy, perfection, or peace from others has erased its possibility from our own lives.

To forgive is to forego carrying one's past identity into the present. It is to lay the groundwork for a change in identity. It is to remove the barricades and the burdens from the face of the present. It is to enter the present day, the present moment, without past hurt and anger and without future plans for dealing with them (ACIM).

To forgive is to enter a moment of spontaneity. Which emotions are spontaneous? Hurt and anger are not spontaneous because they depend on something in the past. Guilt is likewise carried over from the past. Fear is based on misperception from the past which leads to misapprehension of the future. All the happiness we think we've ever had has been dependent on things which have happened to us or that we have made happen. But joy itself is always spontaneous; it is always of the present. To forget the past is to open oneself to the possibility of joy. It is to receive good measure, filled to overflowing.

To harbor anger about the events of the world, about the snags and problems which exasperate us in our relationships, prevents us from sensing the significant depth beneath the surface. To hold anger is to hold the past is to hold back the flood of joy. It is to deny our authentic, deepest self, that self that Jesus manifests and teaches and that he tells us shares the character of God Himself.

'Love your enemies . . . so that you may be sons of your Father who is in heaven; for he makes his sun rise on the evil and on the good, and sends rain on the just and on the unjust.' (Matt. 5:44-45).

'But Love your enemies, . . . and your reward will be great, and you will be sons of the Most High; for he is kind to the ungrateful and the selfish. Be merciful, even as your Father is merciful.' (Luke 6:35-36).

Forgiveness is oversight, but it brings with it insight. Forgiveness looks over the surface in order to look more deeply into the world and the people in it, including oneself. To forgive is to seek another person's potential and to find his or her reality. To forgive is to discover for oneself the easy laughter of those who have overlooked the surface, including the past, and who no longer seek to find their suffering there.

Chapter Six.

The Example of Jesus.

'Every one then who hears these words of mine and does them will be like a wise man who built his house upon the rock; and the rain fell, and the floods came, and the winds blew and beat upon that house, but it did not fall, because it had been founded on the rock.' (Matt. 7:24-25).

And a scribe came up and said to him, 'Teacher, I will follow you wherever you go.' And Jesus said to him, 'Foxes have holes, and birds of the air have nests; but the Son of man has nowhere to lay his head.' (Matt. 8:19-20).

And as he passed on, he saw Levi the son of Alphaeus sitting at the tax office, and he said to him, 'Follow me.' And he rose and followed him. (Mark 2:14)

The Call To Follow.

We have already seen how Jesus not only taught forgiveness, but actively forgave. Similarly, he not only taught about the kingdom of God, he enacted it (Crossan 1994, 93). And, he not only enacted this depth of being, he identified with it; it became his life. Jesus spoke, acted, and lived his life as a participant in another reality.

Jesus taught by example. And his example was to respond to the depth within him. He was the one who decided to identify with this depth, even if the resulting identification made him more than he was, and more even than human.

Having responded to the depth within himself, Jesus was able to ask from that depth for what he needed, to expect it, and to receive it. Through his asking, which is a humbling of himself, he gained in power and effectiveness. It was his ability to ask God for what he wanted and needed, and to expect a favorable response, which made Jesus a "son of God" (Sanders 1993, 161f.).

Jesus asked for and received real power from God, to such an extent that he assumed control over what we consider to be uncontrollable things.

He did not adhere to the laws of the world—even natural laws, the laws of nature which all human beings supposedly must follow. Nor did he accept the social and religious boundaries which he came upon. He was able to surpass the limitations which we feel are an undeniable part of life.

Not only are we entitled to follow Jesus, but we are actively called to do so. The call from Jesus, or the call from depth, is the same now as it was when he was physically present. For the depth of being is essentially the same now as it was then. The same call Jesus heard within himself and imparted to others exists beneath the surface of ourselves.

The call comes from depth, and it is specifically a call to return to depth. The call is the stirring, or awakening, of a dormant potential within ourselves.

A call and an example are given only to those who can follow, to those who have the capacity to follow. It is given to those who can understand, at least potentially. It is given to those who can achieve the same results. And it is given to those who can reach the same eventual destination. An example is given by one human being to others. This is why it helps to see him as a human being in the very same way that we see ourselves as human beings. But Jesus' particular example was given also by one who had surpassed human limitations, at least at times. That is why, on the other hand, it is important to see ourselves as being able to follow him beyond our self-imposed boundaries.

In Jesus' case, an example is a way of life, but, once again, it is not a surface way of life, but a way of life born within, a way of depth. His example is not in the clothes he wore, in the food he ate, or even in the roads he walked. To follow his example is not to do exactly as he did, not even to speak the same words he spoke, but to capture the spirit of what he was and is *in one's own life and through one's own circumstances.*

It is his example which provides the clearest available evidence of who Jesus was. For his teaching can be distorted if it remains outside ourselves. But to follow him is to participate with him. To follow him is to share something of him: it is to share his ideas about life and to apply them in our own lives; it is to share his spirit; and it is to share his mind. It is also to share his "sonship," his ability to ask and receive, his closeness to and familiarity with God.

That having been said, the call does not come from outside us. It may come from outside the selves we think we are, but it does not come from outside of us. Therefore, even if we choose not to respond to it, simply to hear the call is to have one's reality broadened and deepened.

The Call to Gather.

Now the tax collectors and sinners were all drawing near to hear him. And the Pharisees and scribes murmured, saying, 'This man receives sinners and eats with them.'
So he told them this parable: 'What man of you, having a hundred sheep, if he has lost one of them, does not

leave the ninety-nine in the wilderness, and go after the one which is lost, until he finds it? And when he has found it, he lays it on his shoulders, rejoicing. And when he comes home, he calls together his friends and his neighbors, saying to them, "Rejoice with me, for I have found my sheep which was lost."' (Luke 15:1-6).

The surface of the world is a hiding-place for depth. God calls through the world; His call can be heard even through the forms of the world. He calls through the forms of our religion just as He calls through everything else; however, it may be more difficult to hear Him through the forms of our religion if the exterior forms of our religion assume a significance which truly belongs to God, by way of our own depth. Our depth already knows what the surface has forgotten.

The call is always to gather, whether that gathering is done physically, in homes or on the streets, or mentally and emotionally, through forgiveness. Often it begins with the ones nearest you: your family, friends, associates. But this inner sense of community cannot be contained; it begins to extend out to everyone.

The kingdom of God is just such a gathering. It is a communion of individuals. It exists every place on earth where ideas are shared (ACIM), and it exists strongly wherever forgiveness is given and love is shared. It exists, truly, wherever "two or three are gathered" (Matt. 18:20).

The call from depth is also the call to teach. To be called is to be sent out; they are different, seemingly contradictory, aspects of the same motion. It is to say, with Jesus, "'But I have not come of my own accord; he who sent me is true. . .'" (John 7:28). To be called from within is to be sent out specifically to gather, to return to God all that is truly His. The call to teach is the call to join, often through forgiveness.

Jesus came to teach about something beyond himself. As we have seen, he came to teach about the kingdom of God and about forgiveness and about the depth which we keep hidden within us. It was not until later that his followers interpreted this as his having taught about himself, or about their own haphazard but burgeoning communities. Jesus did not come to teach about himself alone. He came specifically to teach about the reality all of us harbor inside ourselves.

Jesus came to teach his followers to be like him. As he is reported to have said, "'A disciple is not above his teacher, but every one when he is fully taught will be like his teacher'" (Luke 6:40). He wanted to give away and therefore share (ACIM) all he had: his calling, his sense of purpose; his effectiveness, his sense of God; and his love, that with which he came to identify.

The earliest Christian communities shared Jesus' example of meeting together for meals. At such meetings, ideas would be exchanged, inspiration would be sparked, and a sense of deeper community would be struck. In the Jewish culture of the time, eating together assumed religious significance. Yet such gatherings were based on something people did every day (i.e., eat and socialize), which helped to emphasize the fact that religion was a part of life which could not be separated out from life.

Simply by sitting with those who were considered sinners, Jesus was teaching them something. For here was a man who was growing in religious authority and influence (at least among the people), who did not behave like a religious authority. For here he sat in their houses, eating with them, speaking with them, treating them as equals. His sense of religion did not call for separating out but for inclusion.

He was gathering them to something higher than they had ever expected for themselves, simply by sitting with them. And of course his words reinforced that he believed that they were meant for something higher, and that they had a depth of potential within themselves which they had yet to recognize. His recognition of it in them evoked it and manifested its reality, just as his recognition and evocation of holiness in the sick brought out the wholeness they held within them. Jesus continually crossed boundaries in order to extend them, and to include within them all who had been excluded.

Finding the Heart.

Jesus answered the call within his religion, which call came from and led back to his own depth. The call is to a broader, deeper reality. It is to see the incomparable grandeur of within where before we could see only the surface. It is to see hope where we once saw only desolation. It is to see life where we used to see only a semblance of life.

What is the essence of Jesus' example? What is it that he did which we can also do? What is it that he did which caused such effectiveness for us?

Jesus belonged to the Jewish religion. This was his religion from birth. That he seemed to interpret his religion so freely, and so differently from many of its first-century authorities, does not mean that he no longer belonged to his religion. What it does mean is that he interpreted it more creatively, and therefore more independently. His great achievement is that somehow he made his religion belong to him. Jesus took the religion into which he happened to have been born, and he revitalized it for himself and his followers.

We do not need to convert to the Jewish religion to follow Jesus, even though he himself never renounced this religion (as many of his followers eventually did), and even though he achieved all that he achieved by following the abiding principles of this religion. Instead, his example shows us that we need to convert *to our own religion.* We need to convert to our own religion in the sense in which William James (the Grandfather of American Psychology) speaks of conversion, as experiencing an increased significance within it and, correspondingly, within ourselves.

Jesus allowed the spirit of reinterpretation to listen through his ears and to reinterpret through his mind and his heart. There are many examples of reinterpretation in the history of Jesus' religious tradition. Abraham and Sarah had faith in that which contradicted what the world told them, and they bore a son in their mature years. Moses did not consent to see his people as slaves but instead knew them as a worthy and Godly people. The Second Isaiah (the prophet who wrote Chapters 40-55 of the Book of Isaiah) made his hope for his homeland real, despite the situation of Babylonian exile in which he found himself.

Thus Jesus continued a tradition of creative reinterpretation into the very heart and soul of his religion. He cleared away some of the persistent overgrowth and then he ventured just a bit beneath the surface. He did not have to dig far before he came upon the depth and the love, the wisdom and the vision and the experience, which lay at its center.

This is what Jesus did. He went to the heart of his religion and he found heart within it. He considered it deeply and he found depth within it. He exemplified its spirit of love, having found love within it.

Jesus reinterpreted passages in the Book of the Prophet Isaiah (in Luke 4:16-21 and 7:19-23), stopping short of the language of condemnation and reciting only the joyous aspects of the prophet's vision (Meier 1994, 134). Similarly, Jesus had followed John the Baptist for a while, but Jesus came to reinterpret the thrust of the Baptist's message from "repentance in the face of imminent doom … to the joy of salvation…" (Meier 1994, 170).

Had Jesus picked up along the way some of the Baptist's fiery, eschatological or world-ending, language, so typical of the ancient prophets and their pronouncements of doom for disobedience? Many people probably believed similarly in the Jewish culture of those times, as opposition to the long period of Roman occupation was intensifying. It is entirely possible that Jesus held an eschatological conception in common with them. It is possible that Jesus believed the world was due to end imminently, but, if he did, it probably had less to do with the prevailing political situation and more to do with the remarkable power being worked through him. If he so believed, then it is another example of the limitations of conception to come to terms with and really to comprehend what Dunn (1975, 89), referring to the inner world of Jesus, calls "the presence of one element, a key characteristic of the end time—the plenitude of the Spirit's power."

Then again, if Jesus believed that the world would end in his generation, it is not likely that he would have suppressed his creative reinterpretation in this one area. Though all the world, and his disciples as well, could believe in a series of concrete happenings surrounding the end-time, Jesus himself could just as well have reinterpreted the multitude of prophecies relating to such events so that they now related to inner events, and to the remarkable power he felt within him and witnessed all around him. For Jesus counseled his followers not to dwell upon the future, "'for tomorrow will be anxious for itself,'" and to focus instead upon the present (Matt. 6:34). As Northrop Frye (197) states, even "a renewal or future restoration is most intelligible as a type of present transcendence."

As an example of Jesus' creative reinterpretation of Scripture in another area, consider his pronouncement against divorce, considered by scholars probably to go back to him in some way. The context of the Gospel narrative has Jesus being tested by some of the religious authorities as to whether divorce was lawful. In reply, Jesus sent them back to Moses (i.e., to the early law), but then had the audacity to counter Moses with his own interpretation of the creation myth in the Book of Genesis, ending with the pronouncement, apparently meant to reveal inner truth, "'What therefore God has joined together, let not man put asunder'" (Mark 10:2-9).

Had Jesus sought to go to the heart of his religion, or had he sought to go to the heart of life itself? Either way, the result was the same. He arrived at a place where religion was intertwined, not with the surface of life, but with the depth of life.

Jesus became the leader of his own religion not because that is what he intended or wanted to do, but rather by a mixture of accident and destiny. Jesus had accepted the elements of his given religion—the ritual, the words, the customs, the laws, even the systems and the authorities—but he reinterpreted the outer elements as inner ones. These elements changed him at the level of depth at which he had accepted them, which is why he was able to allow the spirit within him to reinterpret them for him and for all those he sought to gather and to teach.

Jesus' mission seems not to have been to establish, or even to attempt to establish, outward reforms, whether institutional, social, political, or religious. Even his statements in regard to Jewish religious practices (assuming for the moment that they go back to him) seem to point more toward a re-orientation of inner motivation, of thought and sometimes of feeling, rather than toward a re-organization of the religion itself. Jesus kept his focus upon the inner person, the being who is amenable to depth, the inner person who is able to be saved.

Often, to find the heart of one's religion involves some rein-terpretation of some of the finer points of one's religion. Perhaps this is an individual process—a process between one's religion and one's heart. Perhaps each person who does this does it in his or her own way, and emerges with what seems to outsiders to be a slightly different religion. Yet it is the same religion, at heart.

Even if every person were to reinterpret his or her own religion according to the level of depth found inside, the religion itself would remain the same. It would broaden, it would accommodate more and more, and it would also deepen; the true essence of the religion would be emphasized and the surface elements de-empha-sized. But the religion itself would remain the same religion at heart.

All Jesus did was to take the outer form of his religion and invest it with inner significance. All of religion—as it exists outside and independently of ourselves—is mere form until we take it inside ourselves and thereby render it significant. It is the same with any outside concern: its significance will not be noticed until it is ac-cepted within, there to meet the significance and the depth we hold inside ourselves.

Jesus interpreted his religion personally, through the Spirit's creativity, and he found significance in it for himself. He also found the significance of his religion within himself. And once he had found the heart of his religion within himself, he had, paradoxically, managed—for many who came after—to universalize his religion. And so we benefit from his having personalized/universalized his religion and from his having found its significance within himself and within others. Perhaps it is now up to each of us to follow his example of creative reinterpretation, through the Spirit's power, in our own religion.

A New Way of Seeing.

Jesus states that there is a way of seeing which is "full of light":

> 'Your eye is the lamp of your body; when your eye is sound, your whole body is full of light.... If then your whole body is full of light, having no part dark, it will be wholly bright, as when a lamp with its rays gives you light.' (Luke 11:34, 36).

He suggests that this is the way of seeing which leads to health, for it is the "sound" or whole way of seeing.

If the eye, the faculty for seeing the world, is full of light, then the world is full of light. If the eye is full of light, then the world is illuminated from within.

Jesus was a reinterpreter not only of religion, but of life itself. He can transform our own ordinary perception of the world because he himself perceived the world differently. In his vision, those in the lowest places were now to be considered great; the poor were to be considered blessed; children and the estranged were to be considered at the heart of God's kingdom.

Vision was part of Jesus' example. Without vision, it is said, the people perish. But *with* vision, life becomes more lucid. Even those things which have a tendency to fade away can be reinterpreted, with vision, and saved for generations to come.

Jesus told his followers: "'You are the light of the world'" (Matt. 5:14). This is because he gave them a new way of seeing the world; he gave them vision. It is vision which would grace their works.

Jesus looked and saw not the world we see but the kingdom of God. The Beatitudes may be interpreted as promises of things to come, promises of hope to the hopeless, or they could be seen together as a new way of seeing the world.

> And he lifted up his eyes on his disciples, and said:
> 'Blessed are you poor, for yours is the kingdom of God.

'Blessed are you that hunger now, for you shall be satisfied.

'Blessed are you that weep now, for you shall laugh.' (Luke 6:20-21).

Jesus already saw those poor and lost who flocked to him as blessed. It was not that they would be blessed in some distant future, nor in some world to come. In his eyes, they were already blessed. He perceived something in them which they may have had trouble seeing in themselves. Indeed, he had been one of them. He had seen it in himself first.

But the time for poverty, the time for hunger, and the time for weeping was over, supplanted by light. Vision had come.

Because of their basis in vision, Jesus' words are all geared to the present. They continue to have a certain presence, an immediacy which is difficult to read because our past gets in the way. Only as we free our minds from past interpretations and limitations can we begin to see that the otherworldliness in Jesus' words derived from a depth of vision, a presence, and a light which we could not fathom.

Once we have carried them away from whatever past context we had set them in, Jesus' words will begin to reveal themselves to us in a new light. Once they have convinced us of their truth, they will be newly seen as our own vision and newly heard as our own voice.

A Decision for Life.

The myths about Jesus might be reinterpreted so that we begin to realize that Jesus was not *essentially* different from ourselves; he was not the product of an entirely different order of being. Rather, Jesus was *existentially* different from us—different in terms of the decision he made, and different in terms of the response he made to the call which came from the depth within him.

Decisions of faith are not generally decided upon after having weighed our options consciously and carefully. Such decisions come to us. In a sense, we could say that they are made for us, in our stead, and that we simply follow a set course, a direction that is clear and almost predetermined, and yet not necessarily conscious, not yet anyway, and so it seems as if we are deciding when in reality we are directed in the way we are to go. Such decisions are effortless.

How these and other life decisions come to us when we are ready for them—at the exact moment we are ready to make them or to follow them—it is difficult to know. Like faith, they come to us, assuming our openness to them, when we are ready. We may even struggle at first, trying to decide, but it is only when the struggle is over that we realize how little we have done to make the decision.

The point is that there is something within you which has already decided. In fact, it has never deviated from its original decision, which, in such a case, was never really a decision. The point is that, if we would decide, we must find that part, within ourselves but not of ourselves, and follow it to where it already is. Therefore, we seek the part of ourselves which need not decide, the part which rests above decision and indecision.

The most basic decisions we have ever had to make have all been made for us. And yet they are our own responsibility to make.

Jesus emphasized our own responsibility. It is the belief of those who are healed which really heals them. "'Daughter, your faith has made you well; go in peace'" (Luke 8:48). Jesus is not so much the object of their faith as he is the conduit between their faith, on the one side, and the power of God on the other. Jesus places the focus back upon—and within—the person who believes. It was Jesus' selfless authority which allowed people to believe not only in God, not only in him, but in themselves as well.

The decision he had to make was not quite so simple as deciding who he was going to serve: he had already chosen to serve God and others instead of his surface self. The decision he had to make was whether the vision, the reality that he felt within him and now saw all around him was great enough to overcome even physical reality, life and death. The decision he had to make was whether real life ever really dies, and whether it is dependent on the physical as it seems, whether it is dependent on form for its reality.

Jesus made a decision, and that decision was for life itself. A decision such as the one he made is a decision for a different kind of life than that which normally occupies us. What he showed us—however it actually happened—was that this decision is not voided even by death to the surface. What seems to the surface to be death is not really death, particularly when it is life itself, a decision for depth, which sustains you through existence.

Again, that which looks real on the surface only covers that which Jesus *knew* (eventually) to be real. He retained his faith, his belief in forgiveness, and his hope, which was generally more than hope—it was the present fulfillment of vision.

The surface world pulls us out of our depth even without our continued decision, simply by our own inertia or failure to decide. Our failure to decide leaves us with our default decision, the last decision we have made, even if we have forgotten what decision that was and when it was that we made it. Furthermore, a decision made on and by the surface is really no decision at all. Everyone who lives on the surface has at one time or another opted for the surface, or valued form above all else; for most of us it is safe to say that that was, in effect, our last real decision.

We will remain with form and on the surface until we decide for depth. Fortunately we have the example to follow of one who has already decided for depth and for life.

Jesus chose life. At some point in his existence, he decided for life itself. Long before he carried the physical, literal cross, he had made his decision. Long before he appeared in his risenness to his followers, clothed in a new reality, he had made his decision. Long before he even thought about it, his decision was made.

Most of us never get to such a basic decision as this, and so we continue on in existence, in the world, by our self-concept, in what we call life and death. We choose from among the things we see; our choices are limited by the extent of our vision. Jesus came to teach us that if our vision is not bounded by existence, then neither is our life.

His example was life, not death. His crucifixion was something he took upon himself not to show us how to die, but to reveal how we might live. We might live as witnesses to the same vision that made his crucifixion ultimately become transcended in risen light. We might live with the same certainty, with the same sense of conviction, with the same devotion he displayed in his life (ACIM). We might live with the same vision of forgiveness which illuminates the Passion stories. We might live with the same sense of trust and faith in God.

Whatever the salvific significance Christians might see in the cross, its significance as an example to be followed has been vastly overstated. The Gospels were set up with the crucifixion as their climax. At the time these Gospels were written, or compiled and edited into their present form, circa the year 70 for the earliest of them, Jerusalem itself was under siege and was about to be taken down by Roman forces. The crucifixion then became an example of the persecution the early Christians had to suffer, but it was an example as well of the way to deal with such strife: with patience and with waiting upon the Lord, preferably with transcendence, and ultimately with forgiveness. The early Christians had a model of one who was able to retain the essence, the idea, and the underlying reality of life under the most trying of circumstances.

The cross is the symbol of the transcendence of surface existence, and as such is inextricably linked to the resurrection. Once and for all, Jesus showed the kind of life which has significance for God and for our own depth.

Jesus decided for life, and life became for him more than existence. Life itself took on a universal quality for him. When he spread his arms across the span of the world and cried, "'It is finished'" (John 19:30), it had in reality just begun. His life had taken on a new aspect. He already had the will, the vision, and the self-knowledge to reveal it now to whoever could see and hear him.

Chapter Seven.
That Which Precedes Fullness.

'For what will it profit a man, if he gains the whole world and forfeits his life? Or what shall a man give in return for his life?' (Matt. 16:26).

'Whoever humbles himself like this child, he is the greatest in the kingdom of heaven.' (Matt. 18:4).

'I can do nothing on my own authority; as I hear, I judge; and my judgment is just, because I seek not my own will but the will of him who sent me.' (John 5:30).

The Wilderness.

And he said, 'Abba, Father, all things are possible to thee; remove this cup from me; yet not what I will, but what thou wilt.' (Mark 14:36).

In the Garden of Gethsemane, faced with selflessness, faced with death, he was able to see through that terror and to choose instead the life he felt within him which was not of himself. He may even have resigned himself to non-existence, to being no longer able to help, to heal, to comfort, to save others through his healing and through his forgiveness and through his love. Yet he knew that all along it was not his own will he was following; the will he had come to share was a larger will and a higher will than he could have conceived of alone.

As it turns out, of course, destiny revealing itself perfectly after the fact, he was able to help many more in this way. Despite and through the adversity and isolation he faced, he was glorified. He was vindicated because the higher will he followed was vindicated. His continued existence, even on this earth, was assured. Future events somehow worked out to place his name, and something of his life, into the minds and sometimes the hearts of distant generations. His own effectiveness increased as he was able to give himself to more and more people. His mission, his desire to help, had come to fruition. His desire was great, his will connected with a will not his own; he had a selfless desire, a selfless will, and it achieved more than any self could hope to achieve.

According to what is probably a legend, though probably with at least some basis in fact (mythological if not historical), the earthly mission of Jesus began much as it ended: in isolation. One of the first things that we learn about him, after his baptism and the spiritual experience associated with that, is that he was led by the Spirit out to the wilderness. This is portrayed, in Mark 1, Matthew 4, and Luke 4, as having been his period of temptation in the wilderness.

The baptism of Jesus by John is seen as having revealed the Spirit in Jesus. The Spirit awakened him as of that time, whether or not he was already awake and whether or not it was heard by others at that time. Whereas prior to his baptism by John he might have had a religious impulsion and a decision to make, after his baptism Jesus heard a more direct if not conscious call and leading from within himself, and he felt a "sentness" or purpose coming from beyond himself. Decisions were being made for him.

But the Spirit led him out into the wilderness, into the emptiness and isolation of the wilderness. He could not rest in the fullness of initial spiritual experience. Perhaps it is through emptiness that he learned the glory of fullness. Perhaps it is through isolation that he learned, because he was led by the Spirit, of the need for community.

He had to be led into the wilderness, where not so much the things one has done, as the thoughts one has thought, one's motivations and values, are brought back for reappraisal by no less stern a judge than oneself. Out in the bustle of the marketplace, there is no time to question. But in the stillness of the wilderness there is all the time in the world.

Isolation leaves us with our thoughts. Our vague sense of lack of meaning and motivation and value may appear to torment us at times, but it really rises for our benefit. Such thoughts and/or feelings arise so that they may be judged by ourselves, distinguished, separated out: all that is empty, acknowledged as such and then whisked away by the Wind which knows, and all that remains, to remain as real and as truly valuable.

The devil lies there, in the wilderness, where shadows fall endlessly, but Jesus met him here on a more equal footing. In the world, in the marketplace, he is prince; they are his laws that we regularly, reflexively follow. But here, in the isolation of the desert, no such rules apply. Here, one's eyes are closed to the pressing concerns which make up our daily lives. All the thoughts and feelings of the surface have no worldly object here, except oneself. And if one is honest with oneself, even that is not enough to base one's thoughts and feelings upon.

And that is the point. It is ultimately oneself that one confronts in the wilderness. There is no one here to take the blame for one's own thoughts and feelings. Whatever guilt or shame they may produce is one's own. Whatever decisions one has made in and with one's life are one's own. The major temptation is to ascribe such feelings and such responsibility to someone else, to pass along the blame rather than to deal with the problem where it exists: within oneself.

Who is responsible for tempting us away from depth? Who is responsible for having accepted to live on surface needs and desires alone? We alone are responsible. We have tempted ourselves and swallowed the bait.

Doubt of Everything.

Emptiness might be called doubt of everything. It is not a final doubt, but a preliminary doubt, a doubt leading to something else. We already doubt that a world could be based on joy and on love; we doubt Jesus' teaching, and substitute our own in its stead; we doubt the reality of God's kingdom, the practicality of forgiveness. For this already-doubted reality to rise and to manifest itself, we need to extend that doubt onto the world that we do see, the world we let slip by unquestioned (as to its foundations), our world based on fear.

Why don't we doubt whether this world can make us happy and keep us happy? Has it ever proven that it can do anything more, really, than distract us from the question? All of our faith and trust in the world is based on hope, hope that the world will somehow make us happy in the future, though for now we seem perfectly content merely to chase after a mirage of happiness. As long as we can be distracted by the bustle of the surface from emptiness, and from that which we fear most, which stands just behind emptiness, we go along. Hope for happiness here is as vague a hope as is any hope in an afterlife, and perhaps less warranted.

All things are full of weariness;
    a man cannot utter it;
the eye is not satisfied with seeing,
    nor the ear filled with hearing.
What has been is what will be,
    and what has been done is what will be done;
    and there is nothing new under the sun. (Eccles. 1:8-9).

We believe in the things of the surface. We believe not only in their reality, but in their ability to make us feel certain ways, from happy to sad. To like something is to want to have it, and in a sense to be it; the idea of liking it causes us to want to take it into ourselves. But because it is a surface thing, it cannot be taken all the way into our hearts. Eventually we will come to resent this thing, or even the surface of another person, because its surface, which we like, cannot fill the emptiness which makes us want it in the first place. The power of our passion is strong, as it should be; the surface objects we choose to pour our passion onto cannot hold such strength.

> He who loves money will not be satisfied with money;
> nor he who loves wealth, with gain: this also is vanity.
> When goods increase, they increase who eat them; and
> what gain has their owner but to see them with his eyes?
> (Eccles. 5:10-11).

"The world," spoken of in Jesus' teaching, is that which, if valued for itself, has the power to draw us away from depth. It has the power to draw us away from ourselves. We have given it this power through the value we have seen in it; our valuation is powerful. Therefore, our surface selves have drawn ourselves away from our deeper selves, using the world as go-between.

The world we see and value is a product and reinforcement of a certain conception we hold of ourselves. If we value the surface, that is what we see, and that is what we will become, and how we will begin to think of ourselves. We see and become familiarized with emptiness of all but form. But if we value the depth within both ourselves and others, then we will not live and die with the surface forms.

> Vanity of vanities, says the Preacher, vanity of
> vanities! All is vanity.
> What does man gain by all the toil at which he
> toils under the sun? (Eccles. 1:2-3).

In order to continue to struggle for every scrap of possible happiness we can get, in order to continue to deny the new world and self Jesus held out to his hearers, we need to accept a few preliminary premises. First, we need to believe, against all the evidence at our fingertips, that something outside ourselves can be the key to our inner happiness. Second, we need to forget the doubt that continually creeps in whenever we land back in dissatisfaction. Third, we need actively to forget that all we do here, all we struggle for, all we hope for, and all we finally attain, is fated to follow the way of the surface.

The only life we know of is self-nullifying because it ends in death. Everything tends toward, and eventually meets, its opposite in the world of forms. Every force of growth or becoming which is of this world finds its opposite process of deterioration.

Somehow, however, we sense or intuit that we are built for more. It may be depth that makes us feel, every now and then, that nothing on the surface is enough. Sometimes it occurs to us, for instance: If it does not last, why spend our lives chasing after it? If we are more intent upon the struggle, and do not derive at least one moment of true happiness out of the goal we have attained, then perhaps there is something more worth our little while, and a better way to achieve it. Our heart cries out to hear a calling; our lives cry out for purpose and meaning. To some, and especially to those who counsel surface adjustment, such questioning may seem like a malady. But it may be that it is really a blessing in disguise.

To look at the world more truly, and to see what we are doing here, is to realize that we do not know what we want. For once we have attained what we had been wanting and striving for, we pass through it like a wildfire through dry grass. Given time, our fondest wish and desire is superseded by some other wish or desire; our *psyche*, our depth, it seems, knows that what we wish for is not what we really want. What we really want is something which fills the emptiness of our heart, because the *psyche*, our passion, will not rest with anything less.

If we were to carry into the wilderness only that which we truly love, how much would we take along with us? Would we drag the world with us, or simply let it fade? How much not only of what we already own, but how many of our as yet unfulfilled desires would we pack along with us? And how much of our past, all the memories we think we cherish? How much of ourselves would we really bring? Emptiness answers that question for us. Only those "things" that spark relation truly come away with us. The smallest sense or act of tenderness may prove to be the treasure which sustains a life. Love is truly eternal, and can be sensed as such, when sensed at all, and when contrasted with a sense of the barren backdrop of the world.

Sometimes we sense that something is missing, but even if we stopped to think about it, we would be hard-pressed to know what it is. If there is a treasure hidden somewhere, then it is buried deep, far too deep for us to reach it as long as we hold ourselves to the surface. If there is a solution, or a resource to help resolve this problem, we do not know what it is or where it can be found.

A life preoccupied with the world, and with desires dictated by the world, is a life whose center is somewhere other than itself. It is a life wrangled from itself, no longer naturally-directed, but artificially-directed. Such a life strives for something outside itself to make it feel worthwhile and valuable.

A life separated from its own center and from its own passion, detached from others, and thrown into a world which does not seem to be its own, is a life steeped in fear. An anxious self, consumed with the cares of the world, is a fearful self. The self that must strive must also fear; the self that seeks to acquire or to become anything other than what it is, finds fear.

The Philosopher Martin Heidegger believed that fear "belongs . . . to that inauthentic way of being in which man is absorbed in concern with the world and seeks his security there" (quoted in Macquarrie, 1965, 67). It is the seeking of our security in something which is outside ourselves that keeps us bound to the world, and bound to all that hides life from our eyes.

To counteract being bound to the surface, Heidegger advised the development of a questioning mind, a mind which questions everything, a mind which engages in what he called "meditative thinking." This is a kind of thinking which does not will of itself, but which waits, and asks, and which therefore seeks a will beyond itself (in Long, 64-68). This seems similar to what Jesus counseled, when he told his followers to ask from and for a higher will, to seek what is hidden behind the surface, and to pray.

True Prayer.

How do we find the element which appears to be missing? How do we acquire the depth we need to be as convinced of its existence as we are of the surface world's? Sometimes just asking the question is enough.

Most of our questions have ready responses, conceptual responses which we impose upon the emptiness that might have been fostered by the question itself, had we let it occur. It seems that we are afraid of emptiness, and therefore afraid of questions which have no ready-made, conceptual answers.

Emptiness is really not as fearful as we might think. There is a moment of relaxation in waiting upon an unforced response. There is a moment of relief in the realization that we do not know and need not know everything (in conceptual terms). This is the moment of effortlessness for which we have been waiting; this is the moment of release from constant struggle and even from doubt.

For from the wilderness we can also sense, perhaps only to a small degree at first, where Jesus drew his strength. He drew his strength from what we in the world would call weakness. He drew it from what we in the world would call emptiness. Yet he drew it from truth.

God too can be found in the wilderness, through the Spirit which leads. The Spirit does not lead us into emptiness to leave us there. The Spirit creates a space of emptiness which only God— perhaps in the form of a thought or a feeling, perhaps in the form of a person—can fill.

Jesus continually returned to the social world from the wilderness, and he continually returned to the wilderness from the social world. His moments of solitude, moments of prayer continually restored him to an awareness of God behind the forms, and thus of

God within the world and within the people, and thus of God within himself.

> 'But when you pray, go into your room and shut the door
> and pray to your Father who is in secret; and your Father
> who sees in secret will reward you.' (Matt. 6:6).

Emptiness for Jesus, in the form of the wilderness, in the form of moments of prayer, became fullness. It was this fullness that he poured out upon the world in the form of his teaching, in the form of his way of thinking and feeling.

True prayer is emptiness. True prayer is asking without asking for anything in particular; it is asking without knowing what one wants, asking without knowing what is truly valuable, in order that we might realize that which is truly valuable. That is why we pray, "Thy will be done," rather than our own.

> He was praying in a certain place, and when he ceased,
> one of his disciples said to him, 'Lord, teach us to pray, as
> John taught his disciples.' And he said to them, 'When
> you pray, say:
> 'Father, hallowed be thy name.
> Thy kingdom come.
> Give us each day our daily bread;
> and forgive us our sins,
> for we ourselves forgive every one who is indebted to
> us;
> and lead us not into temptation' (Luke 11:1-4).

Forgiveness is a kind of emptiness, an emptiness of self. As such, it is an appropriate prayer, a prayer which establishes community, a prayer which reveals the kingdom of God. Forgiveness says, "Not my will, but yours," not so much to another person but to God.

Emptiness means emptiness of moral righteousness, emptiness of moral certitude, emptiness of holding any legality or technicality over anyone's head. To be empty of moral righteousness is to ask for a righteousness which comes from beyond ourselves, for it is better to "hunger and thirst for righteousness" (Matt. 5:6) than to believe one already has it.

Emptiness means emptiness of guilt as well. It means emptiness of the past. The moment of prayer is a moment of presence, of suddenness, of immediacy.

True prayer, like a true heavenly reward, does not wait; it is as empty of the future as it is of the past. Only the present, only now, exists in true prayer. The meaning of a heavenly reward is that it is not put off or delayed into an unknowable future. Everything that is knowable is present; it waits within the present moment for us to find it.

Prayer is a giving of oneself to God, not so much in a spirit of renunciation as in a spirit of love. Eventually these moments of prayer build upon themselves, and create a selflessness within a person, a selflessness which allows God to work within and through a person.

> Now as they went on their way, he entered a village; and a woman named Martha received him into her house. And she had a sister called Mary, who sat at the Lord's feet and listened to his teaching. But Martha was distracted with much serving; and she went to him and said, 'Lord, do you not care that my sister has left me to serve alone? Tell her then to help me.' But the Lord answered her, 'Martha, Martha, you are anxious and troubled about many things; one thing is needful. Mary has chosen the good portion, which shall not be taken from her.' (Luke 10:38-42).

When we empty ourselves of all but asking, only the Response remains. Removing all that we have placed in front of it, the Response is free to transform our mind. All that we once considered ours is now freshly considered.

Thought that is deepest springs to mind gracefully and fully-formed from the deepest levels of mind, after the house has been swept out and its dust emptied. Or let the house sit, and be still; the light will find its way within. As it shines upon and through the house, even the dust glitters like diamonds.

Consenting to go into emptiness, we arrive at fullness. Going into the solitude of the desert, of the wilderness, Jesus emerged in the midst of community. Going through the solitude of the cross, Jesus emerged as one with all being.

Going into our own solitude, our own wilderness, we emerge more connected with community. When we left, we left alone. But when we return, we return with all being. And it is all the Spirit's doing; none of it is ours. But of course, if we are one with all being, then what is his is ours as well.

True prayer is emptiness, but it is also watchfulness. "'Watch,'" suggests Jesus, in Mark 13:37. But, as Luke 11:17 states, do not watch the outer world but rather remain awake to your inner world.

To be empty of conceptions is to draw closer to God, because, our conceptions of Him to the contrary, He is not conceivable. He surpasses our understanding, just as His peace does. Conceptions of God make us think we know Him, but we remain at arm's length from Him, while emptiness makes us think we do not know Him, but we end up in His hands.

'Be still, and know that I am God.' (Ps. 46:10).

Ordinary thoughts and desires stand no chance in such an environment of emptiness. Only prayer, an abiding thought, an unconstructed thought, a non-conceptual thought, not detached from feeling, can truly fill an empty heart.

The more we detach from the world, even for just moments at a time, the more valueless the surface ultimately seems (ACIM). That which we once valued is fading fast, because that which possesses real value is rising to the fore.

Still of mind, still of feeling, still of desire, still of resignation: the stillness of prayer is stillness indeed.

Return to the Marketplace.

After his moments of prayer, Jesus returned to the world. He entered the villages of his native Galilee and he entered the homes of whoever would take him in. There are many excuses given later— it had likely caused a minor scandal—as to why Jesus communed with the lost and the estranged, those marginalized from society. The truth is probably that, at the time he set out to teach, these are the only people who would take him in. Only those who feel their own lostness, the emptiness of their heart, are ready for the joyous solution he brings, which we will explore in more depth in the next few chapters. Joy has no meaning to those who believe they are contented with the rising and falling of the surface.

Suffice it to say for now that the emptiness of prayer not only shows us the problem of emptiness at our heart, it also reveals the solution to this emptiness, our fulfillment and our real value.

Why did Jesus return to the marketplace and to society when it was in the wilderness that he found the real problem and the real solution? Because if God could be found in his own heart, then He could be found in the heart of every person. This is why he trusted the human heart. That is why he carried his experience—or it carried him—out into the world. He had his own trust reinforced at the hands of all those who took him to heart, his own experience reaffirmed by all those with whom he could share it.

We have already passed along the problem and responsibility of our own guilt and our own lack of value to other people. We return to the marketplace to gather them back to ourselves, thereby to gather our responsibility. It is by gathering these others whom we have excluded, out of anger or for whatever surface reason, that we gather the lost aspects of ourselves, the fullness we had forgotten. It is by gathering these others that all the lost are eventually returned to their Source together (ACIM).

Why did Jesus continually return to the wilderness when he taught that God was to be found in the marketplace, among daily life and human relationships and even within the business of buying and selling? Because it is only as one finds one's depth that one is able to find God within the surface. It is only by seeing from the depth within oneself that one is able to notice the depth that exists within and among others.

We need to know ourselves in order to know others; then, learning of others, we come to know ourselves better. There is a kind of dialectic—a necessary tension, a working from one side to the other then back again, a realization first within ourselves and then within the other person—in coming to know who we are or who anyone else is at the level of depth. Perhaps we cannot know ourselves alone, and we cannot know others without knowing ourselves, because in truth we are grounded in community, a community of being.

It is the Spirit which led him into the wilderness, the Spirit which led him back into the world, back into the marketplace, where what has been learned can be applied among the forms and the persons we see and believe in.

He carried the emptiness, and the fullness, of the wilderness back with him into the world. Yet as we have seen, and particularly compared to John the Baptist, Jesus was not exactly an ascetic; that is not the way he denied the world. He did not deny it behaviorally, necessarily. He denied it in a deeper way, at the place within the deeper mind where will and desire meet with thoughts (not conceptual thoughts, but foundational thoughts) of value.

Jesus was taken to task for eating and drinking; he was called a glutton and a drunkard (Luke 7:34). He and his disciples were taken to task for not fasting (Mark 2:18). Obviously, Jesus' form of emptiness and of world-denial was other than behavioral, other than ascetic. He denied the world from the point in his mind where desires themselves arise. As always, he got to the heart of the matter.

In some sense, Jesus was estranged from the world; he "had nowhere to lay his head" (Luke 9:58); he was a passerby (Gos. Thom., Log. 42, from Funk, 496). But in another even deeper sense, he was always at home. For it was among people, and particularly among those who may have been similarly estranged, that Jesus really shone.

Jesus denied the world by seeing past it to what there was within it that held real value. One overwhelming value, one inexhaustible treasure, that Jesus found within the world were those people he met with and dined with and spoke with and walked with. He walked with people who may not have shared his realization of depth, but he saw it within them nonetheless, and he revealed to them their own value. And when he looked upon them and within them, deeply from his heart, from the heart of experience, they knew that he valued truly, more truly than they valued themselves.

Form was not a primary concern for him. Thus, if the people he met with had done something in their past for which they felt some shame, he saw directly behind their shame, behind what they had done, to their truth, to their real selves. For the person within the person, the one conscious enough to feel shame, was the same person who was conscious enough to rise above it altogether, and to find him- or herself within the innocence with which one began.

Form was of little concern to him. And so, when he met with people, he did as they did. He ate and drank and talked, but what he talked about, that which came from his heart, was of course different. Empty of moral righteousness, empty of self-righteousness, and empty of self, Jesus was able to transform the lost and the estranged, in his own perception and theirs, into children of God.

What do we do with our former sense of morality and with our persistent desire to judge? Jesus' advice (in the parable in Matt. 13:24-30) was to let all things grow together. Do not attempt to judge now, because your judgment only serves to show that you do not know what it is you do. It is only in the end, once we have grown as mindful of inner depth as we are of outer judgment, that we will begin to see which things grow to fruitfulness and which things will not withstand the strength of our passion.

If we are to renounce anything, such as food or drink, plant or animal, need or desire, it will be renounced for us, by a deeper will than our own. For, as Paul stated:

> I know and am persuaded in the Lord Jesus that nothing is unclean in itself; but it is unclean for any one who thinks it unclean. (Ro. 14:14).

We are not even to judge what is righteousness.

The Value of Emptiness.

Jesus at some point learned to trust that which was leading him. He learned to trust God and he learned to trust his deeper mind. This was what the emptiness and the selflessness of the wilderness taught him.

Perhaps it is a real pleasure, a real relief, to give up the past—to give up our conception of the past, including our past selves, along with all the judgments we have ever made—once we have seen it as it really is.

Our judgments, including our wants and our needs, are persistent; they always seem to come back, even after we had thought they were gone for good. But now that prayer has somewhat disengaged them from us, they no longer lead us astray. Whether we achieve their stated objects or not, we know that it will not be the end of the world. For whether we achieve them or not, we know that these wants and needs will continue to swirl about on the surface, and to rise and fall on their own. They need no help from us one way or the other. They are but distortions of the real passion we can sometimes feel inside ourselves.

Only now, these wants and needs, these desires and urges, suddenly take on a new aspect. Now that we are disengaged from the pursuit, we are able to see that the direction of the everyday is often the same direction in which the Spirit leads, as long as we are willing to learn and to listen. For the Spirit, being resourceful, is able to use anything and everything for His supreme purpose.

Our pilgrimage is here. There is nothing more empty which we might pass through, nothing more wilderness-like, than the multiplicity of forms upon which the surface believes it dwells. Here, within the world and its forms, we are led to learn, first of the emptiness, and then of the truth behind the forms.

Within the emptiness of prayer, we realize that we are being led. After emptiness, everything in the world, perhaps because it now remains somewhat detached from us, has the potential to point the way. And anyone in the world can help us, because we now seem more attached, more conjoined, more connected with her or him due to the depth we feel we share.

It is emptiness which reveals our connection with others. Coming to knowledge of oneself, paradoxically, involves a realization of one's interdependence with others. The more I come to know myself, the more I realize that I need others, that I am not, and never have been, self-sustaining. Nor do I want to return to the surface way of thinking about myself and others, when such depth, and a glimpse of the true promise of happiness, has been embedded in my heart.

Emptiness takes us out of our element, out of the world. It grants us a new context, other than the world, other than ourselves. It leaves us alone with ourselves, but it shows us how to see beyond ourselves.

Emptiness is openness; it is not yet the full view. But in order to receive the full view, we must be open to our part. Our part is merely to clear the slate, or to find the clear state, deep within. Everything else—the grace of fullness—comes from that clarity within.

Now we are led, and led effortlessly, by the things we used to take for granted. After much work is done comes the spontaneity of effortlessness, to complete the work. After a period of much study come creation and intuition. And after emptiness comes blessed fullness.

Chapter Eight.
The Value of Life.

> And he said to his disciples, 'Therefore I tell you, do not be anxious about your life, what you shall eat, nor about your body, what you shall put on. For life is more than food, and the body more than clothing. Consider the ravens: they neither sow nor reap, they have neither storehouse nor barn, and yet God feeds them. Of how much more value are you than the birds.' (Luke 12:22-24).

> 'Consider the lilies, how they grow; they neither toil nor spin, yet I tell you, even Solomon in all his glory was not arrayed like one of these. But if God so clothes the grass which is alive in the field today and tomorrow is thrown into the oven, how much more will he clothe you, O men of little faith!' (Luke 12:27-28).

What is the value of life, of being? Jesus teaches us that there is something more real than the world we see and the self from which we see it. He emphasizes the intrinsic, the inherent value of life, in these passages from Luke 12. In these passages, he is not stressing that human beings are more valuable than animals or flowers—notice in what glowing terms he speaks of the lilies in the field!—rather, he is conveying his belief that human beings are more valuable than we suppose ourselves to be.

We have suffered from a tendency to downgrade ourselves in our own eyes, and to suppose that in Jesus' eyes, and therefore in God's, that we are of little worth. It seems natural now to underestimate ourselves, to deny the worth of our created life. Perhaps we have let our guilt get the best of us, and cover and hide the best we have within us. We have not tried to fulfill the potential Jesus expressed because we did not really believe him when he told us about it. It was easier to believe in him and his potential, him and his grace, than it was to follow him, and believe in ourselves. It is easy to believe in him if what we believe has no real effect, and no real bearing, on ourselves.

To claim that we are hopelessly sinful is to claim that we feel guilty, inadequate, and unworthy. To say that we are fallen from grace is to say that we feel guilty, and cannot reach our natural state of being without help. Even to think that we are estranged from God, or separate from Him in any way, in any aspect of our lives, is to harbor a sense of guilt. We confirm this sense of guilt whenever we judge another, due to interconnection, for it is through our judgment of others that we thereby consent to live our own existence beneath the hawklike eye of judgment and beneath the burden of our own guilt and unworthiness.

Guilt prevents us from seeing life as it is. It makes us afraid to change, afraid to turn around, afraid to go within. It makes us afraid to search in the place (within ourselves) where depth and all that we truly value is to be found. It makes us afraid to come to any real knowledge of ourselves. So we content ourselves to remain with conceptualizations: conceptualized problems (instead of deeply-felt ones) with conceptualized solutions.

Therefore are our beliefs conceptual rather than deeply-felt. Therefore do our beliefs come from our surface minds, and mental logic, rather than from a deeper place. A more abiding sort of belief might actually come from beyond our best formulations; it might be very difficult to fit into words and statements and creeds, being itself alive.

Real Value.

What is the value of life? What if we were to ask, not in order to rattle off some standard and reflexive response, but rather because we do not know, and because we want to know? What if we were to ask because it is our deeply-felt desire not only to know, but to live?

If the value of life is not to be found in food or in clothing, symbols of the surface of existence, then where is it to be found? If a person's "'life does not consist in the abundance of his possessions'" (Luke 12:15), then of what does it consist? If life is not to be found outside oneself, then where is it to be found?

Valuing the outside, the surface, we will search there for life. But to do so is to live without our heart, or with our heart outside ourselves. "'For where your treasure is, there will your heart be also'" (Matt. 6:21). To value instead the inside, the person we are at the depth of ourselves, is to come upon a life which is more truly "us," and more deeply-felt as "ours." It is to live with heart at our center, and it is to see, and to feel an affinity for, and therefore to value the heart in others.

Jesus' teachings shift the locus, the center, of value from the forms of the world to that which is within and yet surpasses these forms. In time, that which is within becomes most highly prized. The values of the world will have been shifted because the reality of the world will have been shifted. Every mind, every heart, and every trace of spirit will be valued for what it is, and valued supremely.

Our passion is not in the right place if it is directed outward. In the Parable of the Spur-of-the-Moment Banquet, those originally invited to the banquet made excuses which had to do with daily living: "I have bought a field, and I must go out and see it," "I have bought five yoke of oxen, and I go to examine them" (Luke 14:18-19). They cannot attend the celebration of life because of the concerns that they have overlain on top of life. To be prudent or merely practical may be somewhat satisfying within its context, but it is no source of joy. Life is a source of joy, not of worry and anxiety and fear, as is the surface all too often.

According to Jesus, we can gain the entire world and lose our life (Mark 8:36), for life itself has little to do with the world. It is not dependent on the world at all, not dependent on the forms we see. As Paul says, "the form of this world is passing away" (1 Corinthians 7:31). Life does not depend on the passing world, but rather on the foundation that God has placed within us. In the words of the prophet:

> All flesh is grass,
>   and all its beauty is like the flower of the field. . . .
> The grass withers, the flower fades;
>   but the word of our God will stand for ever.
> (Isaiah 40:6,8).

To immerse oneself in the surface at the expense of depth is to pay too high a price. To exchange one's very life for all the world is too dear a price to pay. Even to seek for something outside our own depth, the Word that God has implanted in our hearts, is to set oneself up for disappointment when "the [surface] flower fades." Therefore it is the inner depth of the person which Jesus knew to be essential, vital, life-giving, and life itself.

There is nothing in the world which matches our true level of desire because there is nothing in the world which matches our true level of being. But, having made the world our context, we believe we have nowhere else to look. Having made the past our context, we believe we have no one else to be but who we once were, or no one else we could become except that which is based on what we once were.

> Jesus said, 'Become passers-by.' (Gos. Thom., Log. 42, in Robinson, trans., 122).

Yet even our desire, should we follow it where it naturally goes, eventually rises above the world, and above our surface selves, for our desire is too great for the things we feed it. Our desire searches the world for something to fulfill it, to meet it at its level of strength, and it keeps on searching, and it will continue to search until the context within which and from which we search is transformed. It is only within a new context that we will find anything different.

Depth is what we really want; depth is our passion, the heart of our desire. Thus it is somewhat ironic that Christianity has become known largely for legislating against specific desires when, in reality, it is not that we have too much desire but far too little. Our desires for the surface, no matter how pressing they may seem to us at times, do not befit us; ultimately, they are never enough for us. It is too little desire that results in desire for the wrong things, which things are not wrong in and of themselves, but instead because these things do not match the depth of the one who desires them. It is too little desire that results in dissipation, in spreading what little we have around too thinly, in losing what little we have. Even were our desire for the whole of the world, it would not be enough. We need more, and we need it deeply.

Is it any wonder that our wills themselves are feeble and weak, when we have not fed them with the requisite passion? We need to find something of real value, something which carries value in itself.

Objective Value.

'For where your treasure is, there will your heart be also' (Matt. 6:21).

There is something within us which causes us to search. It is a desire for more than the surface has to offer. The potency of our desire burns through the paper-thinness of form too easily. We need to confront this fire within ourselves, but we have no idea how to meet it on its level. Some part of ourselves, it seems, is tired of the things we have made. We need a value which stands as more.

This fire is called the heart, and it knows where its treasure is, but it also knows where it is not. It already knows what it wants, what value is, and apparently will settle for no less.

Where is this ultimate value to be found within the world? What is there within the world that we can love with the whole of ourselves?

> And behold, a lawyer stood up to put him to the test, saying, 'Teacher, what shall I do to inherit eternal life?' He said to him, 'What is written in the law? How do you read?' And he answered, 'You shall love the Lord your God with all your heart, and with all your soul, and with all your strength, and with all your mind; and your neighbor as yourself.' And he said to him, 'You have answered right; do this, and you will live' (Luke 10:25-28).

This is the true extent of how much we are able to value, if we knew ourselves completely. We would be able to value with the whole of ourselves. We would be filled with nothing less than the Ultimate, with God, and with the depth within ourselves and within the other person. Only love is great, great enough to fill us.

Every aspect, every function, every part of ourselves points toward this ultimate value and its fulfillment. Paul Tillich (1957, 114) has called love "the desire and urge towards the reunion of the separated." This yearning for reunion may be the underlying, overarching purpose, and source of urgency, of this burning passion. It may lie at the heart of our need and our strong feelings for other people. It is, at base, a desire to return the inner Word to Him Who has spoken It.

Our true value is given. And that which we truly value is given in the sense that it springs naturally from our heart, our mind, our soul, and our strength—that is, from the whole of ourselves.

According to Robert F. Davidson (173), speaking of the ideas of Rudolf Otto,

> Such values are recognized, immediately and inescapably, as obligatory and objective. They exist in some fashion in their own right, independent of and beyond the control of the individual who acknowledges but does not create them.

And where are such objective values to be encountered? John E. Smith (13) states that:

> In experience we *find* something already there, we *come up against* something, . . . and we do something with the sense that we *undergo* or receive whatever it is that we meet without any sense of being responsible for having produced it.

Once this real presence, this objective value, within ourselves but not of ourselves, is recognized through inner experience, then it will be valued above all else. Our infinite passion can finally rest within an infinite value, namely, the Infinite Itself. Our depth, our heart, will say what it longs to say, with Meister Eckhart (129):

> God is nearer to me than I am to myself. My being depends on God's intimate presence.

This may be close to what Jesus felt, when he stated in John 14:10:

> 'I am in the Father and the Father in me.'

Cares versus Care.

We have strewn most of our cares upon the surface of the world, and we have neglected ourselves and our own depth. Yet Jesus' teaching suggests that *we ourselves* are more valuable than anything that we value in this world. We are more valuable than our constant concern for the world would indicate, more valuable even than all we have striven for and worked so hard to become. For Jesus, our value is not to be found outside ourselves; that is why, in his eyes, the poor are intrinsically as valuable as the rich, the sick as valuable as the healthy, and the sinfully estranged as valuable as the righteous. The surface has absolutely no bearing on the real value of a person.

Life—real life, what the Gospels call 'eternal life'—has nothing to do with outwardness. It has nothing to do with what we ourselves have seen, and everything to do with what and how God sees, and specifically with how God sees us. If we have been following our cares upon the surface, we have not really seen life as of yet. For life comes from within us, where depth is found. Only depth has actual life, according to Jesus.

Jesus' healings were obviously a way of drawing wholeness from beneath surface fracturedness. In his healings, Jesus found something that was more true and more real than the world of appearances, and he drew it from the depth of the person with whom he communed, and it changed the world of appearances. His healings represent, and manifest the effectiveness of, his new way of seeing and valuing a person.

Because his healings are associated with forgiveness, it would seem that what Jesus actually healed was not so much the sickness, but rather the internal rift between the person and God, the alienation, and even the anger, the guilt, and the fear (ACIM). The rift existed as well between the person and the religious community. What is healed, as the "sin," is the sense of estrangement, of separation or alienation, between the person and God. Paul Tillich has stated, "estrangement is what sin means—the power of estrangement from God" (in D. M. Brown, 98). With renewed "faith" in the closeness and care of God, the person was "made whole" from the inside out.

Jesus' teaching was likewise a way of drawing depth, and therefore life, from out of its hiding place. His ideas put forward thoughts which are somehow more real, and feelings which are somehow more true, than those concepts and sentiments upon which we have been feasting and starving. His ideas also propose a sense of community which seems more real than that based upon social factors, a community not of conformists but of individuals who are already whole within themselves.

Once value is found within oneself, it is natural to see it within others as well. Once the surface has been passed over within oneself, it becomes easy to discern the depth within others. Looking from the surface at the surface, our peculiar and fault-finding self-consciousness has led us to seek out the faults of others. We could come up with hundreds of ways in which we ourselves do not measure up to our own standards, should we decide to turn our fault-finding back upon ourselves. But, then, what would be the purpose of that?

We have such guilt inside us. Our judgment of others, and our lofty valuation of the world, both outward-directed thoughts, only serve to reinforce this guilt. There is something inside ourselves which we have been missing, something within for which we have been seeking without knowing how, seeking without knowing what for.

To decide for that something (which is within us yet which comes from beyond ourselves) is to begin to notice its reality in oneself and in other people. To value it enough to decide for it at the level of heart, or with the whole of ourselves (which capacity also seems to come from beyond ourselves), is to make it real for ourselves and for others. Or rather, it is to see its reality, the reality it had before we ever decided. We will spontaneously follow the vision of reality we have chosen.

The worth of the human being is great, and it exists beyond form, beyond behavior, and beyond surface. Our worth, our inner, objective value, could we experience it, would overwhelm our guilt. Jesus spoke of just how great our value is in the eyes of God.

'I will arise and go to my father, and I will say to him, "Father, I have sinned against heaven and before you; I am no longer worthy to be called your son; treat me as one of your hired servants."' And he arose and came to his father. But while he was yet at a distance, his father saw him and had compassion, and ran and embraced him and kissed him. And the son said to him, "Father, I have sinned against heaven and before you; I am no longer worthy to be called your son." But the father said to his servants, "Bring quickly the best robe, and put it on him; and put a ring on his hand, and shoes on his feet; and bring the fatted calf and kill it, and let us eat and make merry; for this my son was dead, and is alive again; he was lost, and is found." (Luke 15:18-24).

That for which we have been seeking is life itself. Created by God, and always in His Hands, we have no idea what it is, no conception which matches its reality. But we have life within us, and we have the means to find it.

Chapter Nine.
The Givenness of Life.

Real Life.

'I came that they may have life, and have it abundantly.'
(John 10:10).

Just as our conceptions of him have never captured Jesus, so
our conceptions of ourselves have never quite captured ourselves.
We have tried to know ourselves through our own limited and self-
referential thoughts, and through our own efforts. But what have we
come to know in this way except our own thoughts reflecting back
at us? In this way we have come to know only conceptions of conceptions of ourselves, based on what we think we've made of ourselves and on what we hope to make of ourselves in the future.

What can liberate us from such reflexiveness? Only truth—
objective, beyond our conceptions of it, beyond whatever we might
make of it—could come in and save us from ourselves, replacing
conceptions and constructions with something more real. It is not
truth in general we are after, not truth in the abstract, but rather the
truth of ourselves: something we can feel and/or experience, something we can live with.

This is the kind of truth that cannot be written down in a book. If we find it there, that is because we have found it in ourselves. If we find it anywhere outside ourselves, that must mean that we have found it within.

The sort of truth we are looking for is life itself, the sort of life which is given us rather than made (or even sustained) in any way by ourselves. It is the sort of life which we might assume had been given us by God, perhaps at some kind of supremely original creation. Yet, however we might conceive of it, this life we seek is more real than any conception of it, more real, because more "given," less constructed, than any label which we might attach to it. It is a pure and immaculate life we seek, untrammeled by our concepts, unspoiled by our guilt, unchanged by the surface.

We look for an identity which is constant, which stands beyond our striving, behind our changes, and which stands before and after our becoming. It stands as a constant because it has been given, not made by us; it comes from beyond whoever it is we think we are. This identity for which we seek stands as a decision, a value, and a reality which has already been made for us and within us.

There is something about a person which cannot be put into words, at least not very handily. The essence of a person is so simple that it seems to our minds to be infinitely complex. It is that essence which, though it were spoken about every day for thousands of years, could never quite be pinned down. The persona, the personality, might be described and characterized and even categorized, but never the person, never the reality.

The reality of a person, the life of a person, can be known only as we know ourselves. Only deep contemplation, and emptiness of everything else, can show it to us. We can only stand back and feel it or experience it as it reveals itself to our attention.

Life is given. It does not come by us but through us. It is given and there is nothing we can do to extinguish it. We can, however, if we wish, replace it in our mind with thoughts and values of our own construction. It returns to us as we give ourselves over to it.

So it depends not upon man's will or exertion, but upon God's mercy. (Romans 9:16).

Givenness.

Jesus' teaching centers on life. He tells us that it is not hard to find, once we know where to look. His teaching is concerned with pointing out where and how to look, and what to look for.

'Salt is good; but if the salt has lost its saltness, how will you season it?' (Mark 9:50).

Saltness is an inherent quality of salt; it is the essence of salt, that which makes it salt. The saltness of the salt is its distinctiveness, or that which makes it salt as opposed to something else. It is so essential to the very reality of salt itself that saltness, as a characteristic, is very hard to describe without referring back to the salt which gives it away. "Saltness" is bound up with (and inside) salt. As such, saltness corresponds to our *givenness*, that which makes us what we are. It has nothing to do with what we think we are, but it has everything to do with who we are in truth.

Where do you look for the saltness, the givenness, the "thisness," of a person? You look beyond her appearance, obviously, beyond her body, beyond her form. For the givenness of a person is not that which passes before our fleeting eyes; rather, the givenness of a person appears to us only as we learn to look from deep inside ourselves. You also look beyond the persona, beyond that scripted and trained part that a person deigns to show to the world. Further, you look beyond who that person might believe himself to be, assuming that he has taken his self-concept from the surface. For the givenness of a person will always seem to match the authenticity we feel whenever we ourselves are able to see ourselves authentically.

'For to him who has will more be given, and he will have abundance; but from him who has not, even what he has will be taken away.' (Matt. 13:12).

This statement takes on a new meaning when it is considered just how much we are given. We have been given much more than we think we are. If we were to attempt to remain content with what we do not have, or with what we have on the surface, even if we have all the world, then we would fade along with it. The life we seek does not fade but instead grows stronger and more powerful as it gains strength from our own value.

It is an entirely new value, and a new life, quite the opposite of what we thought we had, which Jesus urges on his followers. Once we have begun to look for it and caught a glimpse, once we have been given even the slightest taste, our own personal world will never be quite the same. For the beauty and richness of this new life will haunt us until we have uncovered it in all its shining reality. As all the forms of the world dissolve, one by one, or are simply allowed to recede into non-valuation, we continue to gravitate toward this new life.

This new life of which we speak is the treasure which has been hidden from our eyes, for which we would gladly and willingly give up all else. It is the pearl of great value for which the merchant is willing to give up all else, and call it a consummate bargain.

It is the one thing, in or out of this world, which can truly be loved with the whole of oneself—with all of one's mind and all of one's heart and all of one's depth and all of one's strength. There are times when we think we have found something like this, here in the world, but such things always fade, or we change. First the heart, that which wills truly, starts to wander away, and then the mind gradually follows. Such things had never *really* appealed to us because they had never really appealed to our depth.

The kingdom does not fade, but grows increasingly stronger as we realize it more and more. First we get a hint or a trace of experience, a loving thought perhaps, or a losing of oneself in an idea or a feeling which comes from elsewhere. Then that feeling grows, until it occupies our heart and suffuses our minds. And the experience grows, gradually at times, from a hint and a trace to a full-fledged reality, a new life, with a context all its own. It reveals itself more and more until we are convinced of its objective value and eternal nature.

Life does not follow us; it leads and we follow. We do not dictate to life the terms by which we will live; life is its own idea. Life is a larger, greater idea in which we might ourselves abide.

Sonship.

The Gospel of John throughout calls this given life eternal life. The later letter, 1 John, refers to this eternal life as being held 'in the Son.'

> And this is the testimony, that God gave us eternal life, and this life is in his Son. He who has the Son has life; he who has not the Son of God has not life. (5:11-12).

The life that the Son has, which is given us, is similar to the life of God in that it is given, it is "in itself:"

> For as the Father has life in himself, so he has granted the Son to have life in himself. . . . (John 5:26).

To have life in oneself is to have life which exists beyond one's capacity to alter it significantly. A conception (and more than a conception) of life which is real and valuable in and of itself was introduced by Jesus to his followers. And now it belongs to all of us, because it belongs to the Sons and Daughters of God.

It may take a while for the realization to come, but, according to the New Testament, we ourselves are the Sons and Daughters of God. Once our former identity has been bypassed, through emptiness, and we have met up with the objective value and the life within ourselves, then the realization—what it means to be a Child of God—will begin to dawn. In truth, in the eyes of God, we are not at all who we thought we were. What we truly are is given us, but it needs to be uncovered.

'You are the light of the world. A city on a hill cannot be hid.' (Matt. 5:14).

In Johannine theology, it is through our joining with, our receiving of, Jesus that we realize our Sonship.

> But to all who received him, who believed in his name, he gave power to become children of God; who were born, not of blood nor of the will of the flesh nor of the will of man, but of God (John 1:12-13).

Yet Jesus speaks as if the Sonship (and Daugterhood, for gender has been bypassed here) of his followers is a simple, given fact. Jesus encourages his disciples to have as intimate a relationship as he enjoys with God, when he speaks of God as 'your Father' and when he encourages them to call God their Father (as in Matt. 18:14, 23:9; Luke 11:2, 13; 12:30, 32). Dunn (1977, 212) sees by this that Jesus sought to bring his disciples into the same *experienced* reality of Sonship, the same relationship of closeness that Jesus had with the Father.

Paul's participative theology also peaks in Sonship for the believer, often in union with Jesus' Spirit of Sonship. Thus he states that, "because you are sons, God has sent the Spirit of his Son into our hearts, crying 'Abba! Father!'" (Gal. 4:6), and, "all who are led by the Spirit of God are sons of God" (Ro. 8:14).

But it is distinctly in showing, and sharing, the character of God that Jesus tells his followers that they will show themselves to be sons of their Father. For, as John A. T. Robinson (1984, 149) has stated, in much of the New Testament, "to be a son is to show the character, to reproduce the thought and action, of another." The son follows the father, and learns from the father.

> Jesus said to them, 'Truly, truly, I say to you, the Son can do nothing of his own accord, but only what he sees the Father doing; for whatever he does, that the Son does likewise. For the Father loves the Son, and shows him all that he himself is doing...' (John 5:19-20).

For Jesus, what does it mean to show the character of God but to forgive as God forgives?

> 'But love your enemies, and do good, and lend, expecting nothing in return; and your reward will be great; *and you will be the sons of the Most High*; for he is kind to the ungrateful and the selfish. Be merciful even as your Father is merciful' (Luke 6:35-36, emphasis added).

Matthew states the same thing a bit differently, in 5:43-45, 48 (with added emphasis):

> 'You have heard that it was said, "You shall love your neighbor and hate your enemy." But I say to you, Love your enemies and pray for those who persecute you, *so that you may be sons of your Father who is in heaven*; for he makes his sun rise on the evil and on the good, and sends rain on the just and on the unjust.... You, therefore, must be perfect, as your heavenly Father is perfect.'

As Borg (1994, 46) notes, Jesus' teaching emphasized compassion, and this compassion was to be a sharing of the character of God. That is Jesus' message: Be like God. That is the way to follow Jesus, that is the way to be a Son or Daughter of God, and that is the way to life.

To be a Son or Daughter of God is to have life in oneself, a life which has been given once and for all. It cannot be rescinded, and would not be rescinded by God, who gave it to us. We can, like the Prodigal Son, run away from it, and forget its meaning and its reality. But the possibility of return from our self-imposed exile remains forever open.

The Reality Behind Forgiveness.

'And if you had known what this means, "I desire mercy,

and not sacrifice," you would not have condemned the guiltless.' (Matt. 12:7).

To forgive enemies is to have the world re-ordered and our own sense of identity rearranged. It is to see *essentially the same identity* wherever one looks. To commune with the estranged or to pronounce blessing upon the poor is to erase boundary lines which once served to ground our sense of identity. It is to see *essentially the same identity* wherever one looks. All of this boundary-crossing results in the shaking of an already-shaky foundation, and at the same time the uncovering of a timeless and inherently solid one.

Without the usual scapegoats, one must look to oneself, instead of to boundaries and comparisons, for foundation. The foundation, the truth of our being, is covered in judgment, judgment of others which results in a shadow over our own being. If the shadow will not relent, and if judgments seem never to end, then allow the stillness of forgiveness to find the truth in another person, loved one or enemy, and you will not fail to find it in yourself. As Jacques Guillet (97) has stated, forgiveness of our enemy means accepting the fact that the depth, "the secret of his life escapes us," but that we are willing to wait upon God to uncover it for us.

Jesus lifts joining well beyond the level of surface desire or need. It is not what your surface wants or needs from another person that joins you to that other person; it is what you both have inside you. You may not even like this other person, but you are already joined with him or her in a depth perhaps neither of you can yet see. The very fact of your judgment of this other person belies an underlying need to join with him or her, at least at the level of thought. But reaching out to forgive this other, you yourself will realize your forgiveness. It is your joining that reveals the truth about the other person and about yourself.

Our forgiveness of others and God's forgiveness of ourselves are linked in Jesus' teaching because they are linked in our minds. How we treat others and react to others is an unconscious expression of how we feel God thinks about and judges us. Whether we realize it or not, in every action and thought and feeling, we are manifesting who we believe God to be. Is He to be your Care-giver or Judge?

Who He is for others, in our minds, is who He will be for ourselves. Hence the interconnection Jesus taught.

It is only once we have forgotten God that we can judge. Once God is seen differently, can the world seem the same? No, the world is changed; the old world is gone, the new has appeared in its place. The kingdom of God has come, through us, through our forgiveness. It did not fall down from the sky, just as he said it would not. Rather, it came from within us. And it extends automatically from there to all the world.

Forgiveness often seems like a burden to us, a duty, an obligation. But that is because we do not see it from the appropriate context.

> 'Judge not, and you will not be judged; condemn not, and you will not be condemned; forgive, and you will be forgiven; give, and it will be given to you; *good measure, pressed down, shaken together, running over, will be put into your lap.* For the measure you give will be the measure you get back' (Luke 6:37-38, emphasis added).

The potential sadness and unfairness that keeps us from forgiveness seems to be overcome by the tremendous joy and sense of abundance which follows from living in the expansive way Jesus prescribed.

There is joy in forgiveness because there is joy in oneness. One may derive a twisted satisfaction for a time from a sense of superiority or inferiority, but only oneness and equality can produce true joy.

It is through oneness that our true identity is revealed. If one is a child of God, then all are children of God. It is through the manifest reality brought by forgiveness that the community, the collective, the oneness, the equality of the kingdom of God, is entered. For it is when we do not judge, perhaps in a moment of forgetfulness, perhaps out of some deeper will of which we were unaware, that the new world arises in our sight.

And it is only when we realize our oneness with others that perfect forgiveness makes perfect sense to us. It is when we realize our oneness with others that giving is as blessed, because quite the same, as receiving (ACIM). And so, at first we forgive on faith, and soon our reason returns to reinforce it.

To forgive is to realize the oneness of Sonship. It is to realize what Ephesians (4:3, 6) calls "the unity of the Spirit" and the fact that there is "one God and Father of us all, who is above all and through all and in all." To forgive is not even so much to see from the other person's point of view as it is to see from a more-than-human, or Godly, point of view. To forgive is to be like God.

Do unto others as you would have them do unto you. Why? Because you are joined already, at a level of depth and of heart which you learn about as you learn to overlook the surface through forgiveness. What you do to another person is done to yourself; at the level of depth you are aware of this already. Hence, the guilt we sometimes feel when we do something that might hurt another.

Forgiveness leads us past surface distinctions and into a realization of the oneness of creation. Forgiveness returns and restores the innocence of the Sons and Daughters of God. That which forgiveness ultimately shows us is an entirely new reality, which can be seen only with vision, can be told only through revelation, and can be known only by experience.

Jesus' Uniqueness.

How then is Jesus unique, if *all* have it within them to be Sons and Daughters of God, and if all have the capacity *share* with him the character of God, and if all are called to be *one* with him through our forgiveness? Before we answer this question, we should ask ourselves why it is important for us to see him as unique. Is it because we want to be connected with someone who was one-of-a-kind? Is it because we long to be right, so that others might be wrong? Or is it simply because he brings us something different that he is unique?

Generally, when we think of someone as unique, we look toward their characteristics and their greatness of self. But Jesus' uniqueness was not so much a uniqueness of conception as it was a uniqueness beyond conception. He transcended both himself and the world by hearing the call from depth and by consenting to be led there. We may talk about his great independence, his individuality, his authority, his brilliance as teacher or healer, but all of these characteristics, and his uniqueness as well, arise from his incredible selflessness.

Jesus, in his selflessness, was unconcerned with uniqueness of self. Therefore he taught that "'every one when he is fully taught will be like his teacher'" (Luke 6:40). His concern was with the heart and depth of people, not with surface distinctions. That is why he was able to say, when someone was doing good works in his name but was not in the circle of his immediate followers, "'Do not forbid him. . . . For he that is not against us is for us'" (Mark 9:39-40). Therefore it was not the surface that was his concern, but the fact that God's will was done, and done effectively.

It is because of his selflessness that Jesus is unique. For with selflessness came also a remarkable breadth of being: universality of identification.

'Come to me, all who labor and are heavy laden, and I will give you rest. Take my yoke upon you, and learn from me; for I am gentle and lowly in heart, and you will find rest for your souls. For my yoke is easy, and my burden is light' (Matt. 11:28-30).

Here Jesus speaks about joining with all who would join with him, somewhat as a cosmic comforter. Even in his universality, and in the apparent risenness of this passage, Jesus is portrayed as selfless, as "gentle and lowly in heart." Similarly, in the Gospel of John, even as the creative force of the universe and as the link between all persons and the Father, he proclaims selflessly, "I can do nothing on my own authority" (5:30), and "My teaching is not mine, but his who sent me" (7:16).

Jesus was more than himself, but we do not appreciate *how* he was more than himself until we join him in being more than ourselves. Our self-constructed systems cause us to believe we know, intellectually, but he called us to a deeper, more participative knowledge. We have not yet taken ourselves into consideration; we have not yet seen ourselves within his teaching, nor found ourselves in his example, in his life.

And we have yet to find him within ourselves. For, though Jesus may, as theologians claim, represent another order of being, he also represents the depth within us. If he is no longer to be considered *a* human being, that is because he is presently the essence of *every* human being. He is now, not so much what we aspire to be as what we are given to be, somewhere deep in our minds and in our hearts. He is identified with all beings. To see him as he is, then, is to see him as "the true light that enlightens every man" (John 1:9).

Perhaps it is because we have yet to find him in ourselves that we have yet to find him in every other being.

'Truly, I say to you, as you did it to one of the least of these my brethren, you did it to me' (Matt. 25:40).

Jesus identified with the poor, the rejected, the estranged. He included within the circle of God all those who had been left out. That is why he came to be portrayed in such all-inclusive images as the light of the world:

'I am the light of the world; he who follows me will not walk in darkness, but will have the light of life.' (John 8:12);

the living bread from heaven:

'I am the bread of life; he who comes to me shall not hunger, and he who believes in me shall never thirst.' (John 6:35);

the *logos* ("Word") or creative principle of the universe (John 1:1-4); life itself and truth itself (John 11:25; 14:6); and simply eternal being (John 8:58).

It was as a human being that he began to make this universal identification, by stopping in at the lowly homes of the poor and the sick and the despised abodes of sinners and social outcasts. What these later abstract passages in John's Gospel do is simply to emphasize Jesus' human capacity for breadth of identification and care, and to universalize it, as his followers felt his risenness had universalized it, joining him with everyone, including themselves.

Perhaps it is because he identified with so many human beings that he came to be seen as divine being, for he showed his own definition of divinity to be inclusive and encompassing. The seed of abstract and universal identification had been sown in his earthly life. He is now identified with all the world, with everyone we meet, and even with ourselves, within and beyond the participative images used to describe our relationship by the early Christians. Surface distinctions have fallen away; now "Christ is all, and in all" (Colossians 3:11).

What Jesus had to give was something that all of us share; what he gives is that which effects oneness. He gives love, a love which saves and which joins and which returns us to the knowledge of who we are in truth. He returns us to our true life.

> In him was life, and the life was the light of men. (John 1:4).

Even in his humanness, Jesus revealed the nature of life-giving spirit. In fact, it is through his humanness that he was able to speak to those who did not understand their own capacity for transcendence, for spiritual experience. Thus he taught that the beginnings of understanding lay, not in logic or conception, but in something which may seem quite illogical (forgiveness), but which results in emotions which are quite transcendent (love, joy, peace) and which results in a new mind, or a new identity, as well (as a Child of God).

To speak about Jesus is not to speak about him alone, for he was not alone in his earthly life, and he is not alone now. Jesus' uniqueness lay in his willingness to share his uniqueness, and in his willingness to share even his life. His uniqueness stems from the fact that he is, in his risenness as he was in his humanness, a universal being. This makes him no less human, though it does tend to make him more than human. His uniqueness and his greatness come from his human capacity for selflessness and from his more-than-human desire to join himself with all being. The paradox of his uniqueness is that he sought to share it. Therefore his uniqueness is made manifest as we join with him.

Chapter Ten.
Afterword.

The Spirit of Love.

How much are we given? All of our faith, where it is effective, is given; none of it comes from who we have thought ourselves to be. Salvation is utterly effortless.

> 'I sent you to reap that for which you did not labor; others have labored, and you have entered into their labor.' (John 4:38).

> 'No one can receive anything except what is given him from heaven.' (John 3:27).

Love itself comes through us. It is not dependent on anything we do for its being what it is, though we must value it enough to decide to see it as it is. Even our identity is given, not the product of our own construction.

Will our emphasis on the inner life result in a failure to deal with social concerns, with such issues as moral accountability, individual responsibility, and the need for social justice? Would we do

Jesus a greater service by interpreting him according to the legalism upon which the surface loves to dwell, the very legalism against which both Jesus and Paul spoke (e.g., Crossan 1973, 80)? Where do righteousness and responsibility, goodness and justice, come from ultimately? They come from within; they are sparked by the spirit of love which exists within ourselves. Cultivate that first, within yourself, and all the rest will follow. Without that, and without joining with him in that, our accomplishments are scarce.

Jesus' teaching and example is at once a challenge to us and a plea for our own deliverance. We are to be delivered from all that we have constructed, including all of the plans we have constructed for the future of ourselves and of the world, all the legalism which keeps our eyes trained upon the surface (on behavior, for instance), and all the *hubris* or pride that makes us think that we can resolve the very problems that we ourselves have invented.

Legalism, for instance, reinforces our belief that we can make ourselves righteous before God. But the problem is that we have been trying to make ourselves anything at all.

Moreover, legalism causes us to think that the surface is of utmost importance. But if we are not meant for the surface, if the surface is not our destination, then why do we waste our time and effort judging it and picking it apart? If we do not engage our heart, and a mind deeper than the conceptual, then how will we find the peace that surpasses our limited understanding, no matter how diligently we search the surface, no matter how neatly and systematically we have constructed our conclusions?

For Jesus, it was the person that was most important—in ethics as in everything else—not the rule or even the system of rules. As he stated, "'The sabbath was made for man, not man for the sabbath'" (Mark 2:27). The rule, properly seen, is meant to enhance the quality of our lives, not to burden them, nor to entangle us in the legalism of the surface.

It is the heart or the inner being which Jesus emphasizes as the focal point of life. Once we have made it over acts and their consequences, we might stumble upon the roots of something which runs deeper. Once we have made it over, we are free to consider something more, something already set within our heart and deeper mind.

Indeed, for many if not most people conscience already informs them of the rules they need to follow. For most people, to use Paul's words, "what the law requires is written on their hearts" (Romans 2:15). That is, most people follow their own strong sense of right and wrong, even before they are told what is right and what is wrong. Their natural inclination is to do what is right because their natural tendency is to follow the sense of rightness which they can hear and feel within themselves. This is true even if what that person does is not necessarily lawful; I am thinking here again of Paul, who said that he did, not what he knew he should, but what the surface (or "flesh") bid him do (Romans 7:14-25).

The laws of religion reflect our deeper heart—it is from our heart that the laws originally came (Jer. 31:33), just as it is from our heart that all of religion ultimately originated (Otto, via Davidson, 162, who speaks of "a native religious capacity in the individual"). But there is something behind the laws, something more, something more ultimate, that awaits our acknowledgment and return. That something, of course, is love, the deepest feeling of which we are capable, which fulfills the law perfectly (Matt. 22:36-40; Romans 13:8-10).

Morality, as we tend to see it, presents us with a myriad of choices to make—often very difficult choices—and with a variety of situations in which to make these choices. But, as John A. T. Robinson (1963, 112) has stated:

> Jesus never resolves these choices for us: he is content
> with the knowledge that if we have the heart of the matter
> in us, if our eye is single, then love will find the way, its
> own particular way in every individual situation.

This is not only a new morality; it is a new way of seeing.

Our responsibility then, when we look to the laws, is not to find the laws themselves, but rather to find that which is behind the laws, the spirit that fulfills them, the spirit that we are to follow, that intrinsic part of ourselves which conforms most readily with that which we come to realize as a deeper will. If we knew our deeper will, then we would know that what we long for, what we want more than anything else, is to feel a sense of reconnection with God. This is revealed not legalistically or conceptually, but spiritually and rather personally: through the spark of inner experience.

Jesus did not teach the concept of love, but the spirit of love. He did not present us with yet another system painstakingly wrought from the mind of the surface. Jesus did not come to bring us rules to live by, nor even a set of beliefs to write down or memorize. Nor did he come to bring us anything outside ourselves. He presented us instead with the transforming experience of the spirit of love. Jesus came to return us to ourselves.

But legalism will continue to be stressed upon the surface, and people will continue to follow it, and their own freedom will wait on them. For legalism retains the mind we have made, the mind which scans the surface, the mind which judges and hides from judgment. Jesus encouraged instead a mind transformed by depth, a mind which sees from a deeper vision.

The Trust of Jesus.

Jesus entrusted us with our deeper selves. And he entrusted us with depth of vision. But we have forsaken this vision, and have adhered to our former methods of problem-solving. These methods involve adherence to the surface, and to a surface view of things, in order to "fix" the surface, or to construct for ourselves a better world.

Therefore, instead of faith, we have constructs. Instead of a spirit of love, we have laws to follow. And instead of vision, we have problem-solving.

Problem-solving, like legalism, falls back on our former way of seeing. Problem-solving looks for solutions within essentially the same context and conditions out of which the problem arose. It accepts the very principles of the world it seeks to change. It accepts the premises of the conclusions it would like to see overturned. Does this make sense? Does it work?

Social justice, concern for the poor and the marginalized, the outcasts and those without political recourse, all of whom were spoken for by many of Israel's prophets, waits upon our decision. It waits upon our inner decision, our decision to follow rather than to forge ahead without consideration of even the indirect consequences of our actions. For if we pursue our course, even with the best of intentions, and world-wary, but our action results in anything other than love and joining, then it is not likely that our plan will succeed. For if we strive for social (or moral) justice, but forget the inner foundation of social justice, then what we end up with will be, not justice, but a divided house. What we endeavor to do under our own control often ends up out of anyone's control.

Problem-solving douses a fire here while another one catches over there. The problems never go away completely; they change only in appearance (ACIM). Because it sees from the same context from which the problem arose, problem-solving often serves only to reinforce the problem. Jesus' advice was to look first for the inner kingdom, which, when found, will provide one with a new context, all one needs, to solve problems or to do anything else.

'Instead, seek his kingdom, and these things shall be yours
as well.' (Luke 12:31).

That is, the practical things follow from such apparent "impracticalities" as vision, a new way of seeing, and the spirit of love, a new way of thinking and feeling.

The world reflects that which we put into it; it reflects what we give it to reflect. The world reflects how we choose to see, and from where we see, and it reflects how we feel, and from where we feel. If we see, instead of the old world, the kingdom of God, then we have learned to see and feel from the depth which has been given us.

Jesus entrusted to our depth the priceless care of God. It is that feeling, that spiritual feeling, that sense, that spiritual sense, more than any code or organization, that comes down to us today from him. So strong was that feeling that it did not even need to put into words, yet it would still be the underlying reality behind everything he ever said or did. So strong was this feeling behind his words that we can miss the point entirely of the words, and still be held by the feeling.

When he spoke with his Father, he did so in rather intimate terms, confident that God would hear him, though to all the world God was distant, was hidden away. And he spoke with the confidence of a Son, of one who is entitled to speak intimately and directly and fearlessly to God, who had before been imagined frequently as a fearsome Judge.

The same feeling of closeness comes through when he speaks to the world. When he spoke with and proclaimed blessing upon the poor, for instance, he spoke with the confidence, not of one who felt their pain, but of one who saw within them and even shared with them their most glorious moments. Though such moments may have been few indeed, he knew that, by inspiring such moments in them, the intensity of their reality could overspread and even supplant a lifetime of suffering. He did not tell the poor that they would be blessed some time in the future; he told them that they *are* blessed, now, in the vision of the present kingdom of God. Money and social class and religious categorization or the judgment of others had nothing to do with who they are, with who he was, with the care they received in his presence, with grace and with mercy and with blessing. Open your eyes, he said to them, and look upon everything you are given. Look not toward the world for your meaning, but instead to God and to yourself. God denies you nothing—least of all yourselves. The kingdom is in your house and in your hands and in your heart.

Will the love and care of God fail to do what needs to be done? Jesus saw a world we somehow fail to see. It is not that he was a person of special privilege, eternally fated to remain different from the rest of us, created on a better day, with a greater portion of spirit poured out upon him. Nor is it that what he saw was somehow beyond us. Perhaps he simply trusted in love sufficiently to believe in and to ask for and to expect to find this new world, while most often we do not.

Such was the nature of Jesus' "logic," that, he seems to have begun with internal, subjective premises, premises based on inner experience rather than upon external convention. Perhaps it began with an *experience* of what his religion taught him, that God is love; and if God is love, he may have reasoned, then a world of love must exist. And it would follow that this world of love must not be far away, for if God truly loves us, he would not have made a world of love which is impossible to reach or to enter or to receive. The world of love, if it exists, exists in the midst of the present world.

Faith is obviously trust, but trust in what? According to Jesus, faith is trust not only in the reality and existence, not only in the power and might, but in the care and the love of God. Care is basically love, as seen and experienced from the human standpoint. Trust is the ability to overlook anything that would detract from love and from a vision based on love.

Sometimes we seem not to be able to make God care. We seem to be left alone, at least as seen and experienced from the human standpoint. God does not seem to introject His hand into our reality. It is enough to cause us to doubt or even to disbelieve the truth of all those sublime and beautiful Scriptures.

The life and teachings of Jesus suggest to us that sometimes God's lessons are so very simple, so very easy to see, that they may just be missed. It is true that we need to learn of our own responsibility. But it is never true that we learn alone.

Our responsibility just may be to relax and follow His lead. There has never been a time that we have been apart from God. Although at times we may feel that we are utterly alone, completely alone, forsaken, abandoned, there is a way to discern the presence of God even in the midst of this world. Jesus uncovered this presence within himself, probably during many moments in the emptiness of prayer. And he uncovered this same presence in all the world, beginning with the "least" of its inhabitants, during his moments with them.

In Jesus, God and His care do seem to have touched the earth, though not in obvious ways. Where we believe that He has given us a system by which to organize our old thoughts, what He really has provided are new thoughts, inherently ordered, which allow us to see a world which itself is inherently ordered.

Jesus did not speak of or manifest a love which exists only in heaven. That is where it comes from, certainly—its very eternalness can be felt; however, the boundary line between heaven and earth is not as strongly drawn as we might believe. There is a love that exists even in the midst of the pain and self-interest which seem to be our lot here, in the midst of the superficiality and the fading away of all form, even amid all the wrongs which befall us. Jesus spoke of and from a love which reckons the world according to a vision which rises above it, so that our vision can touch and transform and finally transcend the world.

Of Heavenly Things.

'If I have told you earthly things and you do not believe, how can you believe if I tell you heavenly things?' (John 3:12).

The Gospel of John, the least "historical" of the four canonical gospels according to most historians, and the last to be written, rightfully stresses that Jesus was more than himself. The time that this evangelist spent reflecting upon the inner significance—a truth which is other than historical—of Jesus, seems to have been time well spent. For John (or whoever it was who wrote that gospel) speaks of Jesus not from the outside, but from the inside, from the depth and the spirit of the author, which, we are led to believe, is or at least approaches the depth and the spirit of Jesus himself.

The Gospel of John seems to have been based on the premise that it was possible to share the depth and the spirit of Jesus, to know about spiritual things at a level of certainty, to learn about them from firsthand experience. For if Jesus did not derive his own knowledge and insights and power and grace from himself, but rather derived it from a source which approached him from within yet beyond his ordinary self, that is, from the Spirit of God, then it was possible for John to derive his knowledge about Jesus in the same way.

This is something, no doubt, that all of our Scripture writers have felt at one time or another. At one time or another, they had been escorted quite beyond themselves, beyond their past conditioning, beyond their current abilities, beyond even the beliefs and opinions they sometimes held to so fervently, and had come upon an insight which contains a kernel of deeper truth, or a more direct way of communicating that insight to others.

What those inspired Scribes were often trying to express is that we are joined with him, and never again will we split off into our own little worlds, apart from him. For the prayer of Jesus in John 17:20-24 has come to pass (whether we realize it or not):

> 'I do not pray for these only, but also for those who believe in me through their word, that they may all be one; even as thou, Father, art in me, and I in thee, that they also may be in us, so that the world may believe that thou hast sent me. The glory which thou hast given me I have given to them, that they may be one even as we are one, I in them and thou in me, that they may become perfectly one, so that the world may know that thou hast sent me and hast loved them even as thou hast loved me.'

". . . that they may all be one . . . even as we are one, I in them and thou in me, that they may become perfectly one. . .": There is no greater prayer, no higher theology, no more true account of the spirit of Jesus, than this.

Jesus was more than himself, but what we have failed to take into consideration is that he himself trusted that we have it within ourselves to be the more that he was. For we too are more than ourselves, and this is how we must learn to think of ourselves if we are to follow him.

Jesus was more than himself because he was, he became identified with, the depth and value, the love and care of God, which exists in every heart. That is why, no matter how far we may have wandered, we can, if we wish, feel him close by; he is never far away.

One with Self-knowledge.

It is because Jesus had self-knowledge that he seemed to know other people so well. It is not so much that he knew human imperfection and weakness and limitation: these are only surface traits; they do not represent the full range of humanness. The category of humanness does not sit at the opposite pole from that of divinity, for Jesus has shown through his own life that there is at least one point at which the two categories overlap.

In fact, it would make sense to us that Jesus' risenness followed freely and naturally from his humanness. The theology and mythology that came to be attached to him were ways of attempting to explain his risenness, and his risenness was used in turn by the Gospel writers to attempt to explain his earthly life.

There is, we feel, a flow, an interconnection, between Jesus' earthly life and his heavenly life. One does not shine away the other, but instead shines through the other. His risenness can be approached by way of his earthly life. It would be unwise to dismiss his risenness out of hand, due particularly to the effect it had on his followers, whatever the expression of risenness may have been. Just so, it does not help our understanding of him or of faith or of ourselves if we neglect his earthly life, including his teaching and his great effectiveness, in order to hold exclusively to tenets about him.

Had the disciples never seen him and heard him as a human being first of all, how would they have been prepared to see him and hear him in his risenness? As Jesus is portrayed as having asked in John 3:12: "'If I have told you earthly things and you do not believe, how can you believe if I tell you heavenly things?'"

The best category we could come up with to explain the person of Jesus was that of divinity. That says something not only about him, but about ourselves as well. For Jesus, if indeed fully human as theologians suggest, extends the range of humanity. The tide lifts every one of us, at least in potential. The true significance of this fact will surge beyond our "common knowledge" and reveal to us what *inspiration* really means. We will know it when we are ready for it and when we have asked for it from the depth of our heart.

At times, our little life gives way to something greater, and we feel and eventually come to know that this something greater is more real, and more close to us, than is the little life which is eventually left behind. Sometimes we ourselves give way to the greater life of an idea, an idea which can be shared, an idea which joins, and which can grow and increase of itself. Even in the world, our individual lives often cede to the community—ideally an all-inclusive place in which ideas, like feelings, are shared and communicated, a community characterized by oneness, a community similar to what some might envision as the kingdom of God.

The point of Jesus' story is not that he lowered himself to our level, the level at which we believe we exist. The point of his story, instead, is that he appeared at our level in order to show us that we can raise ourselves, or be raised, to his level. That we have taken his story to mean that we are as low as he is high says that we would rather remain (or see ourselves as remaining) in limitation, for the time being. But if indeed we can see ourselves as he did, as the Gospels suggest and state that we can, then perhaps we can also be transformed, here and now, once and for all; perhaps we can also learn to be who we really are at or near the level of depth and of spirit in which Jesus lived.

That returns us to the theme of this book: The way to understand Jesus (from within) is to approach his level of depth within ourselves, and then to remain open when this depth, which is in but not of us, reveals itself through us.

The story of Jesus is our story; it is all of ours. It is not his alone. He himself belongs to every individual; he is the model individual, the paragon, the exemplar. Though others have their own paths to God and to themselves and need not follow him specifically, he belongs to everyone. He also belongs to God. Thus does he show us where we, as individuals, belong.

What about the myths which have become a part of his story? He did not originate the myths about his past, but he did inspire them, through the way he lived his life. All of those who have picked up his spirit have carried on this legacy, one way or another, both inside and outside of the churches he inspired but never established,

including the countless churches not made with hands, which oc-
cupy the hearts of individuals everywhere.

The myth about Jesus began in the heavens, with a bright
star, which was seen and followed by wise men and simple shep-
herds. What the star promised was universal salvation. It promised
a final reunion, not so much accomplished by one person as led by
him and his Spirit. And the final joining would be, and will be, and
is already, in him.

What occurred within that starlight may be believed, but it
is not *necessary* to believe it in order to believe in, to see, and to be
affected by Jesus' divinity. The myth works in its context, within
the person, where the message of Jesus' life and teaching works.
What is most significant for us is the decision he made, which was
not a decision to become divine, but rather a decision to allow divine
love to fulfill itself through him. A historical account of his earthly
life need not disregard the influence of spirit, or at least of something deeper than that for which history can provide explanation.
Even our legalistic interpretations of him have not chased away his
spirit. For to have the myth or the person work in you is to be opened
to a new level of literal truth, which just so happens to be spiritual
truth. It is truly to be born again. It is to see all things anew, as if
from above. It is to be saved, liberated, redeemed, and delivered,
delivered to where we belong in truth.

Bibliography

All Bible passages are from the *Revised Standard Version Bible: An Ecumenical Edition*, copyright 1946, 1957, and 1971, by the Division of Christian Education of the National Council of Churches of Christ in the U.S.A.

Anonymous. *A Course in Miracles* (ACIM). Tiburon, CA: Foundation for Inner Peace, 1975.

Blakney, Raymond B., trans. *Meister Eckhart: A Modern Translation.* New York: Harper Torchbooks, 1941.

Borg, Marcus J. *Jesus: A New Vision.* HarperSanFrancisco, 1987.

-----. *Meeting Jesus Again for the First Time.* San Francisco: HarperSanFrancisco/HarperCollins, 1994.

Brown, D. Mackenzie. *Ultimate Concern: Tillich in Dialogue.* New York/Evanston/London: Harper and Row, 1965.

Brown, Raymond E., S. S. *An Introduction to New Testament Christology.* New York/Mahwah, NJ: Paulist Press, 1994.

Brown, Schuyler. *The Origins of Christianity: A Historical Introduction to the New Testament.* New York: Oxford UP, 1984.

Crossan, John Dominic. *In Parables: The Challenge of the Historical Jesus.* San Francisco: Harper and Row, 1973, pap. 1985.

-----. *Jesus: A Revolutionary Biography.* San Francisco: HarperSanFrancisco/HarperCollins, 1994.

Davidson, Robert F. *Rudolf Otto's Interpretation of Religion.* Princeton, NJ: Princeton UP, 1947.

Davies, Stevan L. *Jesus the Healer: Possession, Trance, and the Origins of Christianity.* New York: Continuum, 1995.

Dodd, C. H. *The Founder of Christianity.* New York: Macmillan, 1970.

Dunn, James D. G. *Jesus and the Spirit.* Philadelphia: Westminster Press, 1975.

-----. *Jesus' Call to Discipleship.* Cambridge/New York: Cambridge UP, 1992.

-----. *Unity and Diversity in the New Testament.* Philadelphia: Westminster Press, 1977.

Frye, Northrop. *The Great Code: The Bible and Literature.* San Diego/ New York/London: Harvest/Harcourt Brace Jovanovich, Publishers, 1982.

Funk, Robert W., Roy W. Hoover, and the Jesus Seminar. *The Five Gospels: The Search for the Authentic Words of Jesus.* Poleridge Press/ Macmillan, 1993.

Gilkey, Langdon. "The New Being and Christology" in *The Thought of Paul Tillich.* Eds., James Luther Adams, Wilhelm Pauck, Roger Lincoln Shinn. San Francisco: Harper and Row, 1985.

Guillet, Jacques, S. J. *The Consciousness of Jesus.* Edmond Bonin, trans. New York/Paramus/Toronto: Newman Press, 1971.

Hopper, Stanley Romaine. *The Way of Transfiguration: Religious Imagination as Theopoesis.* R. Melvin Keiser and Tony Stoneburner, eds. Louisville: Westminster/John Knox Press, 1992.

James, William. *The Varieties of Religious Experience: A Study in Human Nature.* New York: Mentor/New American Library, 1902.

Jeremias, Joachim. *Re-discovering the Parables.* S. H. Hook, trans. New York: Scribner, 1996.

Jung, Carl G. *The Undiscovered Self.* R. F. C. Hull, trans. Boston/Toronto: Little, Brown and Co., 1957.

Johnson, Luke Timothy. *The Real Jesus: The Misguided Quest for the Historical Jesus and the Truth of the Traditional Gospels.* San Francisco: HarperSanFrancisco/HarperCollins, 1996.

Kee, Howard Clark. *Understanding the New Testament*. Englewood Cliffs, NJ: Prentice-Hall, 1983.

Koester, Helmut, and James M. Robinson. *Trajectories through Early Christianity*. Philadelphia: Fortress Press, 1971.

Long, Eugene Thomas. *Existence, Being and God: An Introduction to the Philosophical Theology of John Macquarrie*. New York: Paragon House, 1985.

Louth, Andrew. *The Origins of the Christian Mystical Tradition: From Plato to Denys*. Oxford, NY: Clarendon Press/Oxford UP, 1981, rep. 1985.

Mack, Burton L. *The Lost Gospel: The Book of Q and Christian Origins*. San Francisco: HarperSanFrancisco, 1993.

-----. *A Myth of Innocence: Mark and Christian Origins*. Philadelphia: Fortress Press, 1988.

Macquarrie, John. *An Existentialist Theology: A Comparison of Heidegger and Bultmann*. New York and Evanston: Harper Torchbooks, 1955.

McCormick, Scott, Jr. *Behold the Man: Re-reading Gospels, Re-humanizing Jesus*. New York: Continuum, 1994.

Meier, John P. *A Marginal Jew: Rethinking the Historical Jesus. Vol. 1: The Roots of the Problem and the Person*. New York: Doubleday, 1991.

-----. *A Marginal Jew: Rethinking the Historical Jesus. Vol. 2: Mentor, Message, and Miracles*. New York/London/Toronto/Sydney/Auckland: Doubleday, 1994.

Moulé, C. F. D. *The Origin of Christology*. Cambridge/London/NY/Melbourne: Cambridge UP, 1977.

Otto, Rudolf. *The Idea of the Holy*. John W. Harvey, trans. London/Oxford/New York: Oxford UP, 1923, pap. 1958.

-----. *The Kingdom of God and the Son of Man: A Study in the History of Religion*. Floyd V. Filson and Bertram Lee Woolf, trans. Grand Rapids, MI: Zondervan, 1937.

Patterson, Stephen J. "Sources for a Life of Jesus" in *The Search for Jesus: Modern Scholarship Looks at the Gospels*. Washington, D.C.: Biblical Archeology Society, 1994.

Robinson, James M., et al., trans., *The Nag Hammadi Library in English*. San Francisco: Harper and Row, 1977.

Robinson, John A. T. *Honest to God*. Philadelphia: The Westminster Press, 1963.

-----. *Twelve More New Testament Studies*. London: SCM Press Ltd., 1984.

Sanders, E. P. *The Historical Figure of Jesus*. New York/London: Allen Lane/Penguin Press, 1993.

-----. *Jesus and Judaism*. Philadelphia: Fortress, 1985.

Sanford, John A. *The Kingdom Within: The Inner Meaning of Jesus' Sayings*. San Francisco: Harper and Row, 1987 (revised edition).

Smith, John E. *Experience and God*. New York: Oxford UP, 1968.

Smith, Wilfred Cantwell. *Faith and Belief*. Princeton, NJ: Princeton UP, 1979.

-----. *The Meaning and End of Religion: A New Approach to the Religious Traditions of Mankind*. New York: Mentor/New American Library, 1963.

Tillich, Paul. *Dynamics of Faith*. New York: Harper and Row/Torchbooks, 1957.

-----. *The Eternal Now*. New York: Charles Scribner's Sons, 1963.

Trigg, Joseph Wilson. *Origen: The Bible and Philosophy in the Third-century Church*. Atlanta: John Knox Press, 1983.

Wilson, A. N. *Jesus*. New York, London: W. W. Norton, 1992.

Index